W9-AVB-703

COMPARATIVE LEGAL CULTURES

PRENTICE-HALL
CONTEMPORARY COMPARATIVE POLITICS SERIES
JOSEPH LaPALOMBARA, Editor

published

forthcoming

HENRY W. EHRMANN

Prentice-Hall, Inc.
Englewood Cliffs, N.J.

COMPARATIVE LEGAL CULTURES

Library of Congress Cataloging in Publication Data

Ehrmann, Henry Walter
    Comparative legal cultures.

    (Prentice-Hall contemporary comparative politics
series)
    Bibliography: p.
    Includes index.
    1. Comparative law. I. Title.
Law   340'.2   75-31815
ISBN 0-13-153858-6

COMPARATIVE LEGAL CULTURES
Henry W. Ehrmann

© 1976 by Prentice-Hall, Inc., Englewood Cliffs, New Jersey

All rights reserved.
No part of this book may be reproduced
in any form or by any means without permission
in writing from the publisher.

Printed in the United States of America

10 9 8 7 6 5 4 3 2 1

PRENTICE-HALL INTERNATIONAL, INC., London
PRENTICE-HALL OF AUSTRALIA, PTY. LTD., Sydney
PRENTICE-HALL OF CANADA, LTD., Toronto
PRENTICE-HALL OF INDIA PRIVATE LIMITED, New Delhi
PRENTICE-HALL OF JAPAN, INC., Tokyo
PRENTICE-HALL OF SOUTHEAST ASIA (PTE.) LTD., Singapore

To the memory of
Wolfgang G. Friedmann, 1907–1972

fellow-student in Berlin,
and in exile
a source of inspiration
to all students of comparative legal thought
and institutions.

CONTENTS

FOREWORD

The series in Contemporary Comparative Politics is unabashedly committed to several goals. We assume that the undergraduate student is by and large not interested in becoming a political scientist but is planning to follow other pursuits. This being so, we aim to expose these students to aspects of politics that will be salient to them throughout their lives. In order to make this point stick though, we believe it is necessary to avoid using the so-called "grand theories" of political science as organizing frameworks. Such "theories" are subtle forms of misinformation; they mislead students—and sometimes others —into believing that we know more about political systems and processes than is actually the case.

It is also our assumption that only the rare undergraduate wishes to master the workings of any single political system. Even where such interest may be present, the study of single countries rarely leads to anything resembling systematic comparative analysis. Therefore, we have sought to focus on a wide range of interesting and important aspects of politics that individual volumes in this series treat comparatively.

We also believe that those aspects of politics included in this series should be treated from both an institutional and a behavioral perspective. Political science will remain a hobbled discipline as long as those who write or consume it elect one of these orientations or the other. Political science will become or remain an arid discipline if we neglect to treat the normative side of politics. The authors of this series are neither bare-facts empiricists nor "cloud-ninety" political moralists. They are prepared to use whatever forms of comparative analysis are available to permit us better to understand the relationships between political institutions, behavior, values, and man's condition. The range of understanding we seek to achieve is reflected in the core of this series (Joseph LaPalombara, *Politics within Nations*) and in the titles of individual series volumes.

Because no series can encompass all areas of politics, we have had to make choices. Some of these choices will introduce the reader to aspects of politics not often treated on a comparative basis. Our published volumes on political violence and corruption, and a forthcoming book on the military in politics, fall into this category. Other choices will expose the reader to more traditional aspects of government and politics treated in a fresh comparative perspective. Series volumes on national legislatures, bureaucracy, political elites, and elections are designed to fall into this category.

In many ways, this volume by Henry Ehrmann follows both guidelines. It is a short book on the role of law in the governance of nation-states, and Ehrmann's learned, probing treatment of this important but neglected aspect of political science is in itself an important innovation.

This is also a book about legal cultures, a comparative analysis of the ways in which a variety of nation-states have confronted the problems of welding together a reasonably well-integrated national political system. Ehrmann's treatment gives us unusual insights into the ways in which a variety of political relationships, political institutions, and individual and group behavior are conditioned, influenced, and circumscribed by the law, legal institutions, and experts in the interpretation of the law.

If this book achieves the impact we intend, it should serve as a model for additional research and analysis into this vitally important aspect of politics. In the nature of things one scholar can cover only a limited number of the extant and still-growing number of nation-states. Henry Ehrmann has cut a path that many should follow and expand in directions that lead to greater illumination regarding the relationship between law and politics in many other societies. Such intellectual forays will open up new vistas from which to make better assessments of the roles of lawmakers, lawyers, judges, and eventually law enforcement agencies and officials in the dynamics and the problem-solving capabilities of nations.

New Haven

JOSEPH LAPALOMBARA

PREFACE

This book is the outgrowth of an undergraduate course in political science which I have taught for many years at various institutions. Entitled "Comparative Jurisprudence and Legal Philosophy," the course proposed to study the lawyer's quest for a systematic vision of legal rules, and the philosopher's effort to understand the role of the legal order in his and any society.

Students and colleagues seemed to agree that there was room for such an addition to the curriculum (beyond the conjectured benefits for students seeking admission to law school). Legal and political philosophy are intertwined at many points; yet courses in political philosophy generally leave little room to the thoughts on law of even the most prominent political philosophers. Courses in comparative politics may discuss the judicial branch of government, but they are usually short on exploring the manifold legal aspects of community life.

When Joseph LaPalombara suggested that I develop for the present series that part of the course which was primarily comparative and leave aside a discussion of the broader philosophical issues, my hesitations were twofold. I was concerned that such a cleaving would deprive the book of some of the contemporary "relevance" which students had discovered in the great philosophical controversies of past and present. Imposed space limitations created additional difficulties. How would it be possible to compare in a meaningful way a great variety of legal systems in less than two hundred pages without confusing the readers presumably unfamiliar with most of what law is about?

In order to overcome these quandaries I have geared pertinent materials to certain concepts that have been developed and used, admittedly with uneven results, in comparative politics and political sociology. Hence the student for whom this book is the first brush with "legal science" should be able to relate novel situations to familiar sights and to discover analogies between the functioning of legal and other political institutions.

Also the general approach chosen here should be familiar to the student of comparative government: it is functional in an almost elementary, if methodologically eclectic, way. The inquiry focuses on what the law and those who operate it *do* to and for society, to and for human beings. Because any functional analysis is bound to seek an explanation for the frequent disparity between promise and performance of legal systems, it cannot and should not avoid a discussion of the ends of law in different societies. Hence comparison leads of necessity to an examination of the values and interests represented or violated by the law. Driven out by the front door, legal philosophy finds ways of intruding into any comparative inquiry.

A discussion of the basic concept of legal culture, as I have used it here, must be reserved to the text. Readers will have to decide whether it has enough explanatory force to be truly useful for an analysis of differences and similarities, of surprising convergences and stubborn divergencies. The trail I have taken has been broken quite recently by a number of younger scholars (as my references will show). But my attempt to apply the notion of legal culture to a great variety of contemporary legal institutions and practices can be nothing more than an "essay": I have indicated at many points how much more we need to know to transform hunches into valid hypotheses, to say nothing about solid evidence.

If the "multi-national" bibliography appears overrich for a book of modest size, there are two explanations: (1) For many of my (tentative) conclusions I have relied entirely and quite intentionally on the findings of others; the references to my legal readings of half a lifetime acknowledge this. (2) Students, and perhaps other readers as well, should become aware of the rich opportunities, some of them as yet uncharted, that exist for pursuing an exciting field of comparative studies.

My gratefulness to other than "printed sources" is sincere and I am indebted to many—first of all to the many hundreds of students who have enrolled over the years in my jurisprudence course and who by their interest and inquisitiveness have compelled me to revise constantly notes and thoughts. The manuscript was read with great care by my French colleagues M. Pierre Laroque of the Conseil d'État and M. André Tunc of the Université de Paris, and in the United States by my colleagues and friends Donald MacNemar of Dartmouth and Joseph LaPalombara of Yale. Their suggestions for improvements and clarification were invaluable.

The manuscript was typed efficiently by Mme. Raffard of Paris, the first truly bilingual secretary I have had the privilege of knowing. Calvin C. Jones, student of Government 51 when I taught it for the last time at

Dartmouth, labored with skill and diligence over the references and the bibliography; he has almost convinced me of the virtues of a computerized bibliography.

The book was in part written and entirely rewritten during a year of residence and teaching in Paris. Throughout our sojourn the unfailing hospitality of our friends Marcel and Françoise Merle and of their family was a boon to intellectual productivity and greatly added to our joie de vivre.

Hanover, N.H.   HENRY W. EHRMANN

COMPARATIVE LEGAL CULTURES

LEGAL CULTURE
ITS
DETERMINANTS,
ITS
COMPARABILITY

1

THE DEVELOPMENT OF LEGAL CULTURES

This book sets out to heed Hobbes's recommendation of "applying reason" to the study of law by studying both more and less than the "common laws" of a single or of several countries. Its principal focus is the comparison of *contemporary* legal cultures. Their historical development will be treated only incidentally. However, by way of introduction, a few near-universal traits of legal history are sketched here in order to illustrate the place of law in the ever ongoing contest between tradition and modernity.

Primitive law is fascinating, and not only for the anthropologist, because it demonstrates that binding rules that govern conduct can exist before there are specialized organs for their creation and enforcement. Although law cannot develop without the existence of a community, the community does not need to have the characteristics of a state to give itself legal rules. When norms to which no sanctions are attached prove defective because they cannot solve uncertainties as to the existence or the scope of the norm, the community will seek to attach such sanctions to behavior of which it disapproves. Therewith a corner is turned: society has stepped from a prelegal into a legal stage.[1]

The German sociologist Max Weber has rightly stressed the absence of sharp boundaries around what should be called legal:

> *Law, convention, and usage belong to the same continuum with imperceptible transitions leading from one to the other. . . . It is entirely a question of terminology and convenience at which point of this continuum*

[1] Selznick, 1968, p. 52.

>   *one shall assume the existence of the subjective conception of a "legal obligation."* [2]

At first the determination, the adjudication, and the enforcement of accepted norms will often remain decentralized. Anthropologists have pointed out correctly that it is wrong to define the forces of law in terms of a central authority, of courts and constables. As long as such authorities are lacking it is left to the members of the community, be they individuals or groups, to seek satisfaction from the lawbreakers by retaliation, blood feud, enslavement, and similar means.

But all the time and in accordance with changes in the society, the human concerns affected by law will gradually become broader. On its long march through social institutions the legal system will gradually overcome decentralization until at the end of this development unity, uniformity, and universality will be regarded as the characteristic traits of a modern legal culture.

"Law, being a practical thing," a great American judge has stated, "must found itself on actual forces." This implies that legal development is inseparable from changes in the underlying societal institutions as well as from the changing feelings and demands of the community. A European scholar, a pathbreaker in the field of comparative legal sociology, summarized his empirical findings by explaining that "the center of gravity of legal development lies not in legislation, nor in juristic science, nor in judicial decision, but in society itself." [3]

It is true that these statements are too broad to pierce some of the mysteries about the interaction of social norms and legal rules. Legal relations, such as exist between father and son, buyer and seller, creditor and debtor, and rulers and subjects, can hardly be observed, let alone evaluated, over time except against the background of social activities in which these relations are functioning. [4]

The law of feudal societies was vastly different from that of primitive peoples. Yet legal relations were still a web of privileges for some and of protection for others; rules were particular rather than general; and unequal treatment was accepted as the price to be paid for membership in the legal community. This situation changed when the state, by revolution or reform, replaced the autonomous jurisdictions of an estate society by a nationwide jurisdiction. [5] At least in theory the hallmark of a sovereign state,

---

[2] Quoted here from Abel, 1974, pp. 221–22; see Abel, 1974, p. 223 for what follows in the text.

[3] See Holmes, 1881, p. 213 and Ehrlich (1912), 1936, p. xv.

[4] Radcliffe-Brown, 1952, p. 181.

and by implication of modernity, was the unlimited authority to edict laws and to provide for the authentic interpretation of their meaning.[5]

At the same time the position of the individual within the legal order was transformed. After the breakdown of feudal society and the frequently spurious protections it offered, equality before the law meant that the individual was left alone and that he had to face the wealthy and powerful through the give-and-take of supposedly freely entered agreements. The state machinery was standing by to enforce, through its courts, compliance with the obligations that had been assumed. During long stretches of the nineteenth century, appropriate legislation, outlawing associations such as trade unions, saw to it that the individual remained isolated.

Even before the onrush of social problems and the ensuing maladjustments compelled new changes in the law, the operation of the "legal" system was frequently not as uniform as was claimed in the capital cities of modern nations or colonial empires. A sociological view of the law will always distinguish between the law on the books and the law in action. To judge a legal system by the text of its statutory enactments and by the rules governing court procedures would give a distorted picture of the results it produces in life. Discrepancies between what is prescribed and expected and between what occurs in fact exist everywhere.

Ordinarily changes in the law will be slower than changes in society. Alterations in the economic structure, in social manners, in traditional beliefs, or even in the sense of justice do not generally express themselves immediately in an alteration of legal rules. To bring about changes in the law it is generally necessary that social and political pressures be built up, and even after this appears to have been done the pressures can be deflected or arrested unless they are strong and specific enough.

In times of real and perceived emergencies, of major technological breakthroughs, of social catastrophies and widespread indignation, law will make the jump that enables it to confirm or even accelerate social change. In certain situations a legal elite or another power group might introduce changes in the law that are ahead of public opinion. Gaps created in such a way are particularly great where an urban elite attempts to impose its legal concepts on a custom-bound peasant society. This was equally true in a colonial situation, such as the British attempt to come to terms with the Hindu and Moslem legal traditions in India, and in the far-flung Habsburg empire before the First World War. However, there also exists in highly modernized and seemingly more homogeneous societies a hiatus between legal ideals and reality. Under certain conditions, largely determined by

---

[5] For an excellent and comprehensive treatment of these developments, see Bendix, *The Few and the Many,* forthcoming.

the existing legal cultures or subcultures, such discrepancies are accepted passively for a long time. But the moment might come, when the law by the very expectations it has raised mobilizes enough energies to provide a vehicle for actual rather than merely promised change.[6]

The question of whether law can and should lead or whether it should never do more than cautiously follow changes in public sentiment has been and remains controversial. The British social reformer Jeremy Bentham and a German legal scholar Friedrich Karl von Savigny have provided contrasting paradigms for these propositions.[7] At the outset of the age of industrialization and urbanization, Bentham expected legal reforms to respond quickly to new social needs and indeed to restructure society. He did not hesitate to tender advice to the leaders of the French Revolution since in his opinion countries at a similar stage of economic development needed similar remedies for their common problems. Writing at about the same period, Savigny condemned the sweeping legal reforms that the French Revolution had introduced and that were threatening to invade continental Europe. In his opinion only fully developed popular customs could form the basis of legal change. Since customs grow out of the habits and beliefs of concrete people, rather than expressing those of an abstract humanity, legal mutations could only be national, never universal. Savigny had formulated his theory for a practical political purpose: he was opposed to the introduction of the newly codified French law into the German states. But much earlier, a Frenchman who, because of his insight into the interdependency of law and other social factors, can be considered as the father of comparative legal sociology, had expressed similar scepticism about the suitability of one nation's legal system for another. On the basis of his studies of the relationship among law, physical and cultural conditions, and the form of government, Montesquieu had concluded that since laws must harmonize with the general conditions of a country, they would never be valid outside of the country for which they had been created.[8]

As our further discussions will show, neither Bentham's faith in the emancipating force of universal legal developments nor Savigny's cautious reference to the Volksgeist, the spirit of a people, describes correctly the reality of evolving legal cultures. There have been frequent migrations of legal institutions from one culture to another. Such grafting has been totally or partially successful when the need for reform arose out of material or ideological needs and when the indigenous culture offered no or only

---

[6] See Selznick, 1968, p. 57.

[7] These writers and their contrasting views are discussed by Friedmann 1972, pp. 19f., and Friedmann, 1967, pp. 209–13 (Savigny) and pp. 312–20 (Bentham).

[8] Montesquieu (1753) 1949, Book I, pp. 6–7, and Book XIX, pp. 307–15.

insufficient methods of handling the new situation. (The fate of the jury system in different national settings, to be discussed below in Chapter 5, will provide one of many illustrations.) Although ideas never pay import duties, the penetration of legal rules and institutions resembles the situation in which economic goods are imported: the imports might upset the national economy, but such a, possibly temporary, imbalance must be evaluated against the likely privations of autarky.

In recent times pressures generated in some of the most highly industrialized and bureaucratized societies have provoked legal developments that appear to move away from the tenets of the modern state. Legal privileges are bestowed on nonstate organizations such as powerful associations and interest groups. Because of the information they possess they have become seemingly indispensable for the rule-making by either parliament or bureaucracy, which in turn has permitted them to play an active role in setting priorities for legal reforms. They also are relied upon to provide remedies for the overburdening of a centralized judicial apparatus by taking into their own hands the settlement of legal disputes of an ever-widening range (for details, see below Chapter 6).

To the individual these groups and associations provide legal protections that the laissez-faire state had denied him; but he also finds himself limited in ways that resemble those of an earlier feudal order. He no longer needs to bargain singly about the conditions of his employment. But he also can no longer obtain housing, utilities, insurance, or credit at conditions he might personally choose. The form contract and its small print eliminate such choices and determine the status of those in need of services. In 1861 the British legal historian Henry Maine observed that "the movement of the progressive societies has hitherto been a movement from Status to Contract." [9] Since Maine wrote this, modern legal culture has in many respects reversed its course and reinstated us in the Procrustean bed of status. The sovereignty of the state has in some important repects again given way to a web of decentralized legal communities.

THE CONCEPT OF LEGAL CULTURE

A study like the present one that settles on the concept of legal culture as a focus for comparison is bound to define what is meant by it. The student of comparative politics will ask about the connections between legal culture and political culture, a notion that, in recent years, has won widespread acceptance because of its promise for producing a satisfactory explanation of many aspects of political life. Anthropologists and sociologists have done more than admit the profusion of meanings attached to the term "culture," which to them is as

[9] Maine (1861), 1916, p. 174.

complex as it is important. They have also bequeathed their uncertainties to other social scientists who are searching for categories that would prove useful in cross-national research. How to distinguish culture from society, from its institutions and overall organization, how to decide whether culture systems are the products of action or whether and to what extent they condition further action, how to prevent the concept from becoming a mere abstraction and therefore losing some of its usefulness for empirical research —these are some of the questions that have been raised in the literature without having been satisfactorily answered.[10] Nonetheless there is sufficient agreement on the main ideas the term embraces to discern the particular place of law among them.

Culture results from the association of human beings, and it makes their association possible. It outfits men with more than their anatomical endowment. However, for enabling them to live in society, culture exacts as its price for protection a variable amount of conformity; it insists that the members of the society assume definite obligations.

Some of these obligations—for example, a certain amount of respect for the life of others, a curb on continuous physical violence—are common to all human associations. Others are peculiar to that "fragment of humanity," the single culture which "presents significant discontinuities in relation to the rest of humanity." [11] Single cultures acquire their specificity from the natural and human resources which are at their disposal and from the experiences which each culture has made in the process of solving its particular problems.

Problem-solving activities, taking into account the failures and successes of the past, create defined patterns of thought and of beliefs; through them future actions are led into established grooves. Hence all culture patterns must be cumulative and historical. Once established they might be able to outlive the specific societal conditions from which they had originated.

As a design for societal living culture provides potential and actual guides for the behavior of the accultured individuals. A knowledge of cultural patterns, whether or not they are tied to specific institutions, permits one to gauge the persistence of traditions and to discern the likely modes of change. For individuals and groups will add to the traditions by technical and social inventions or by novel combinations of previously separate traditions. Ingenious inventions of this kind are particularly frequent in the field of law.

The thought and actions of its members will inform the basic postulates of a society and shape the principles, the usually unquestioned premises,

---

[10] The wide varieties of approaches are discussed critically by Malinowski, 1931, pp. 621–45 and, a generation of scholars later, by Singer, 1968, pp. 527–43.

[11] Lévi-Strauss, 1963, p. 295.

which govern the social order. Traditional behavior secretes rules for future behavior; yet the rules may vary with the real or perceived needs of the society. All societies draw such rules from fields that are, in most systems, categorized as morals, religion, ethics, etiquette, customs, and laws. When, why, and under which historical conditions a society will abstract legal rules from the universe of postulates will be discussed frequently in this book. For the present it is sufficient to state that even when specifically legal rules have emerged they continue to draw their substance and form from other cultural postulates and, like all postulates, from life itself. Compared with morals, laws has a more definite structure. Like language it lives on as a group of symbols by which cultural patterns are transmitted. And also like language, legal rules express the solidarity traits of a definite fragment of human society which might be identical with or larger or smaller than the nation state.

The relationship between economic and social solidarity and legal rules might be illustrated by the role of the canoe, an artifact whose cultural identity anthropologists have often discussed. Whether the canoe is manned by a single person or a group, or whether it is owned individually or collectively, it creates relationships which in turn rely on a bundle of rights and obligations. But the latter are linked with social organization possibly long before any body, privileged to establish public law, has come into existence.

However important the environment and the conditions of production and distribution of goods are for the development of appropriate rules, these are not the only factors which determine cultural postulates and legal traditions. The relations among men—attitudes of deference or expectations of equality, trust or distrust, indeed some basic if not always explicit concept of human nature—all have an impact on the role of law in society. In different systems and at different periods that role might be paramount or secondary; its relative importance might shrink or grow when compared with other ways of regulating human behavior. Yet in primitive as well as in developed societies the legal culture remains an important vehicle for transmitting traditions of behavior.

For a writer who uses the concept of "legal tradition" in much the same way as this book speaks of legal culture, a legal tradition is

> a set of deeply rooted, historically conditioned attitudes about the nature of law, about the role of law in the society and the polity, about the proper organization and operation of a legal system, and about the way law is or should be made, applied, studied, perfected, and taught. The legal tradition relates the legal system to the culture of which it is a partial expression.[12]

[12] Merryman, 1969, p. 2.

Another author distinguishes the cultural elements in a fully developed legal system as

> *the values and attitudes which bind the system together, and which de-termine the place of the legal system in the culture of the society as a whole. What kind of training and habits do lawyers and judges have? What do people think of law? Do groups or individuals willingly go to court? For what purposes do people turn to lawyers; for what purposes do they make use of other officials and intermediaries? Is there respect for law, government and tradition? What is the relationship between class struc-ture and the use or nonuse of legal institutions? What informal social controls exist in addition to or in place of formal ones? Who prefers which kind of controls, and why?* [13]

If these are the questions which the study of legal cultures intends to answer, it is obvious that a close relationship exists between the concepts of legal and political culture. Students of political culture have chosen from among the various meanings of culture the psychological orientation of individuals and groups. Attitudes towards the political system and its insti-tutions have been categorized into cognitive, affective, and evaluative or normative dimensions; they define the situations in which political action takes place.[14] When used with caution the concept has proven quite useful for comparative analysis. By considering political culture as the link between what happens in the mind of individuals and how political institutions func-tion, one may be able to bridge the gap between the study of the individual in his political context and the political system as a whole.

Legal culture also functions as such a link. The attitudes, beliefs, and emotions of the operators as well as of the users (and victims) of the legal system have much to do with the way in which it functions. Most citizens have a less distinct knowledge about the outputs of the legal system than they do about politics. Opinions concerning desirable ways for legal insti-tutions to operate might be vague and generally less emotional than opinions about political symbols and institutions. At any rate some of the usual tools of political analysis, such as public-opinion and attitude surveys, will rarely provide satisfactory data for this field. But somewhat aimless feelings about "there ought to be a law" can run high in some societies (in the United States, among others). The like or dislike for specific legal institutions will

---

[13] Friedman, 1969, p. 19.

[14] The foremost works discussing the concept of political culture are Beer and Ulam, 1973, pp. 25ff.; Almond and Verba, 1963, esp. chaps. 1 and 12; and Pye and Verba, 1965.

always be linked to traditions and to the culture in which the legal system is embedded.

From this perspective both the political and the legal culture may be viewed as subsystems of their cultural environment. But both of these systems harbor their own subdivision: there is a political as well as a legal subculture of the urban ghetto or of the isolated villages in a rapidly modernizing country. Just as in some systems the army or the militants of a radical party live in a political subculture of their own, the judicial or another legal subsystem might live apart and occasionally clash with values prevalent in the society.

If it is true that political institutions and processes can survive only when the socialization of a substantial number of the citizenry into the political culture has been successful, a parallel and simultaneous socialization into the legal culture must also take place. The learning process might vary in intensity and use a variety of channels. Besides the informal and formal education provided by home and schools the encounter with reality—that is, with the police, with the no-trespassing signs of various kinds (actual or symbolic), and with the courts—might intensify the knowledge, if not always the acceptance of prevalent values and norms. The mass media, in newspaper reports of crime and punishment or court-room scenes in films, for instance, provide a distorted but nonetheless effective image.

Political socialization prepares individuals for their recruitment into a variety of political roles such as participants in mass demonstrations, as voters, as members or activists in parties and pressure groups, or as leaders. At first sight recruitment into the legal culture seems to prepare for little more than the acceptance of the system. In a field such as the law where the division of labor has developed in most cultures a high degree of specialization of an operative elite, recruitment into an active role appears quantitatively strictly limited. But an important aspect of general socialization into the legal culture should not be overlooked and will be discussed below (see especially Chapter 5): litigation, the appeal to the courts, is nothing less than participation in legal life. Different cultures socialize their citizens into either engaging in or avoiding legal contests by the judicial process and, more generally, into making the appropriate choices for dispute resolution. In some countries, including the United States, certain minority groups which lack electoral strength find it more profitable to resort to litigation rather than to legislation. In such situations the judicial process provides a forum for raising issues in a different context from the one provided by legislative or executive decision.[15] To be involved in such "class actions" before a court or administrative tribunal is an effective experience of social-

[15] Peltason, 1968, p. 288.

ization and occasionally one which leads into assuming a more active role in legal *and* political culture.

THE VARIETY OF LEGAL CULTURES

Although the careful study of a single legal culture can yield valuable insights, only the analysis of a variety of legal cultures will recognize what is accidental rather than necessary, what is permanent rather than changeable in legal norms and legal agencies, and what characterizes the beliefs underlying both. The law of a single culture will take for granted the ethical theory on which it is grounded. But when we observe different cultures which embody different ethical theories and which use such beliefs to produce different legal results, we are able to distinguish the respective places which ethical rules, legal norms, or other techniques of social control hold in different societies.[16] Questions which in one society are deemed legal "by nature," might be categorized and treated differently elsewhere. Hence comparison induces the self-reflection that leads to the fuller understanding of even a single system.

Early in the nineteenth century a legal philosopher who was also a practitioner of the law urged his contemporaries to venture into the comparative field:

> *Why does the legal scholar [he asked] not yet have a comparative jurisprudence? The richest source of all discoveries in every empirical science is comparison and combination. Only by manifold contrasts the contrary becomes completely clear; only by the observation of similarities and differences and the reasons for both may the peculiarity and inner nature of each thing be thoroughly established. Just as from the comparison of languages the philosophy of language, the science of linguistics itself, is produced; so from the comparison of the laws and legal customs of nations of all times and places, both the most nearly related and the most remote, is produced universal jurisprudence, the pure science of laws, which alone can infuse real and vigorous life into the specific legal science of any particular country.*[17]

In his enterprise the student of legal cultures risks the same pitfalls as the political scientist or sociologist engaged in the comparison of different systems. He might be misled by the similarity of terms and legal concepts or by the outward resemblance of institutions. What he needs to study instead are the *functional equivalents* in various cultures. He must start

---

[16] See Northrop, 1959, p. 184, and, comprehensively on a sociologically informed comparative legal science, Kahn-Freund, 1962, pp. 368ff.

[17] Anselm Feuerbach, here quoted from Berman, 1959, p. 560.

with a legal problem of social significance, such as the payment of debts or the relief of victims of unfair competition, and seek to discover the rules or institutions by which these problems are resolved from one system to the other.[18] A leading student of legal anthropology has identified four basic "law jobs" common to most societies (and the realist school of jurisprudence has adopted his analysis): social control, conflict resolution, adaptation and social change, and norm enforcement.[19] By which institutions and which methods are these law jobs performed? Which of them are emphasized or relatively neglected in different cultures? How does the law, which is always multifunctional, satisfy or frustrate the felt needs of the community? And what must be compared functionally must not be pronouncements, however solemn, nor statutes, however precise, but actual results.

All comparison proceeds from classification, and it is indeed possible to distinguish various "families" of legal cultures which have survived a secular process of assimilation and of slowly growing universality of habits, techniques, and mentality. Classifications of legal system are hampered by the fact that law, like nature, does not submit to sharply divided and mutually exclusive categorization. There is for instance no modern system that relies entirely on statutes, none that is entirely unwritten or to be found exclusively in court decisions. In regard to some legal relations, for instance those of a constitutional nature or norms regulating the transfer of landed property and succession at death, a given system might belong to one family, but when it comes to contracts and torts it resembles another category. The frequent phenomenon of imitating (for good or bad reasons, by choice or by force) foreign legal institutions might lead to a hybrid system which defies classification. That it might nonetheless be valid and dynamic is demonstrated in our time by the private law of Israel which contains elements of Talmudic, Islamic, Roman-Catholic, canon, and Ottoman law.

In some countries a deliberate selection of norms imported from another family of legal cultures has been used to bolster indigenous institutions which otherwise would have become obsolete. In other situations the native and the imported systems may compete with each other and the outcome, rather than outward appearances or styles of judicial decisions, should determine the proper categorization. In a new environment a foreign legal device might often be so thoroughly transformed that, contrary to intentions, the legal system continues to function essentially according to previous traditions. But in some, admittedly infrequent, situations a deliberate onrush of new legislation might crash traditions and move the system from one group to another as has been the case in modern Turkey

18 See Rheinstein, 1968, p. 208.

19 Hoebel, 1954, pp. 10ff.

and Japan. Highly industrialized and urbanized countries such as, for instance, Great Britain and Germany, will find similar solutions to their nearly identical legal problems. They might still use some methods that have grown out of traditions congenial to the legal family to which they belonged. Yet the similarity of results would lead a functional comparison to the conclusion that earlier categorizations are all but devoid of interest.

These and other reservations concerning the construction of useful models must be kept in mind if one seeks to arrive at an ordered classification of legal cultures. The one adopted here [20] has found fairly wide acceptance although other models have claimed greater sophistication or comprehensiveness.

The families distinguished here will be:

1. the Romano-Germanic family;
2. the family of the common law;
3. the family of the socialist laws; and
4. the non-Western legal families.

The last category appears the least satisfactory, and on the face of it, patently Western-ethnocentric. But it is a fact that in our century the three systems of Western origin have spread over the entire world and are transforming the once-differing legal cultures of Asia and Africa. In the field of law, and for reasons yet to be discussed, modernization and "Westernization" are more closely connected than in political or economic development.

The Romano-Germanic Family   This family includes those countries in which legal science, and with it important elements of legal culture, have developed on the basis of Roman law. Formed in continental Europe, it is still principally centered there today although it has been modified substantially in Communist Europe. On the other hand many non-European countries have not only borrowed from it but have sometimes adopted in its entirety what is referred to here and elsewhere briefly as the "civil law." [21] All of Latin America belongs to this family; in North America the legal system of "New France," which is today the Canadian province of Quebec, and the state of Louisiana adhere in some essential part to the Romano-Germanic traditions, as do many of the states that were formerly French colonies in Africa and Asia.

---

[20] It follows in all essentials David and Brierley, 1968. But see also Friedmann, 1967, pp. 515ff.

[21] The term "civil law," here used as a description of the codified systems of continental Europe as distinguished from the English "common law," is sometimes also used as a translation of the *droit civil* or private law as distinguished from public law.

The first comprehensive compilation of the rules of any legal culture was undertaken in the sixth century A.D. under the Roman emperor Justinian; it furnished the foundations and thereby influenced the future development of all of the systems of the Romano-Germanic family. The labors carried out upon the orders of Justinian were as significant as those which the modern codifier Napoleon was to direct in similarly authoritarian fashion. Justinian's compilations combined rationality and abstractness with great flexibility by entrusting to the legal profession the pragmatic application and the development of the principles they had announced. Due also to the efforts of the universities in both Romanic and Germanic countries the basic concepts were adapted over time to changing conditions. That this was greatly facilitated by the use of a common language—Latin—demonstrates the close connection between verbal and legal symbols.

Early in the nineteenth century the Napoleonic codes brought a new systematization and therewith an even closer affinity to the legal systems of this family. In the important field of private law the Code of the new German Empire of 1900 and the Swiss Code of 1907 introduced modernized versions that were to compete with the French Civil Code. Similarities of and differences between these codes are the result of conscious imitation here and of innovation there. Singly or in combination they have been taken as models by other countries throughout the civil-law world. Because of their compact, almost "packaged" form codes have proven quite suitable for export from one country to another. One writer has correctly characterized this process as a form of mild conquest radiating from an intellectual accomplishment across national borders.[22] It has mitigated the effects of legal particularism and nationalism in many nations, although the courts of the various nations have frequently imparted different cultural traditions in their interpretation of the norms. Hence identical codes have occasionally produced contrasting results. If all of the civil-law countries share a common legal heritage, they do so to a different degree.

In a cultural perspective the survival of the civil law in Quebec (through the instrumentalities of both a Civil Code and a Code of Civil Procedures) is of particular interest. To the legal elites of the province the norms as well as the spirit of these codes are as indispensable for the cultural identity of Quebec as the French language, and must in their opinion remain intact. In spite of some slight incursion of English private law no major difficulties arise as long as the settlement of legal disputes remains in the hands of provincial courts. However, when cases are brought from there either to the Privy Council in London or, since that appeal was abolished, to the Canadian Supreme Court, difficulties could result from the

---

[22] So Schlesinger, 1959, p. 265.

fact that judges from other provinces who are strangers to the language, the manners, and the usages of the Quebec law will have a part in the final decision. These difficulties are paralleled by the fact that the French-speaking judges on the Supreme Court have to hear cases that come from the rest of Canada. In fact, most observers believe that this dual system has not given rise to major difficulties: even though the reasoning of the two groups of judges may occasionally have been different, they always reach the same results.[23] This can be taken as important evidence of the rapprochement of the civil- and the common-law systems in the present age. In Louisiana the existence of a civil code, patterned after the French example, has not prevented the legal cultures of the state, the working laws of social and economic life, from being replete with common-law elements. Louisiana lawyers are seldom able to read French legal materials, and this is an additional factor in making the law of the state much like that of the neighboring states.[24]

In continental Western Europe special legal traditions have survived in regions which for geographical or historical reasons have remained isolated, such as certain Swiss cantons and the Scandinavian countries. The law of the Scandinavian countries is not codified to the same extent as that of other countries belonging to the Romano-Germanic family. Earlier compilations of customary laws had made comprehensive modern codifications less urgent. Widely divergent constitutional and legal developments, rather than cultural differences, are making it in fact difficult to assign all of the Scandinavian countries to the same or any legal family.[25]

The Family of the Common Law   This family includes the legal system of England and those systems modeled on the English law: the systems of the United States, the countries of the British Commonwealth, and the former British colonies. When, beginning with the Norman Conquest, it became incumbent on the royal judges to declare the law of England, they considered it their foremost task to settle individual disputes rather than to develop general principles for future conduct. For being less generalized their rulings were also less abstract than those made by their brethren on the continent. Legal science as developed at various European universities had little meaning for the business before them. But that also meant that, with some not altogether unimportant exceptions, the sweep of the Roman law was halted at the channel.

The legal systems of the United States and of some Commonwealth

---

[23] Russell, 1969, pp. 216f.

[24] Friedman, 1969, p. 35.

[25] David and Brierley, 1968, p. 41.

countries have gone their own ways; in some fields the differences between their law and the English law are as pronounced as those between various countries belonging to the Romano-Germanic family. Yet feelings that family ties are binding the common-law world together are not merely sentimental: judicial decisions reached in one system still have persuasive authority and may be quoted in those of another. The major differences that exist, especially between the English and the American law, emerge on a more fundamental and cultural level: they concern the role which the members of the society attribute to the law as a vehicle for conflict resolution as well as the nature of the judicial process and will be dealt with in detail below (especially in Chapters 3, 4, and 5).

Scottish law presents its own anomalies to the common-law world. Even though linked with England through centuries of political union and sharing with it in the House of Lords a common supreme court, Scotland has kept laws that were strongly influenced by Roman law. The mentality of the Scottish jurists has remained akin to the more abstract reasoning of their continental colleagues and yields different results in certain fields.

A comparison of the legal life in Anglo-American and Western European systems is particularly rewarding. Grounded in different historical traditions the law in all of these countries had to reckon with similar economic, social, and technological developments; moreover through long stretches of time most of these countries have shared political ideologies. Hence the differences that remain, while exaggerated by some and slighted by others, must derive from variations in the legal culture which will be discussed throughout this book.

The Family of Socialist Laws [26]   In the first years after the Bolshevik revolution Soviet society tried to live by the principle that communism, having abolished the antagonism of classes, was not to mean the victory of socialist laws but the victory of socialism over any law. In a society where for centuries formal law had been significant only in the relationships of a small elite while the masses of the people lived by customs and bowed to discretionary rulings of the powerful, the announced withering away of all law meant nothing shocking. Yet with the introduction of the New Economic Policy in 1921 earlier views had to be revised and it was soon proclaimed that under socialism law was to be raised to the highest level of development.

In terminology, concepts, and structure the Soviet codes and statutes, like the czarist law before 1917, have many affinities with the legal systems of the Romano-Germanic family. From a sociological viewpoint, however, the nationalization of the means of production changes the nature of the

[26] The most comprehensive and up-to-date treatment of fourteen systems of socialist law is that by Hazard, 1969.

law rather thoroughly in spite of the fact that the Soviet laws regulate contracts and legacies and provide for orderly court procedures. Everywhere legal institutions have a political purpose. But by making this explicit and reminding its publics of it on every occasion, the Soviet system has given to the agencies involved with the legal life of the country characteristics different from those generally accepted in the West.

Although all the Peoples' Republics in Eastern Europe now belong to the family of socialist legal systems, they have not adopted carbon copies of the Soviet law. In some of them civil-law traditions had stronger roots than in czarist Russia, and in countries from which far fewer lawyers have emigrated than from the Soviet Union, the influence of the civil-law trained professional lawyers has not entirely lost its impact. Moreover none of these countries experimented, as the Soviet Union had done, with the abolition of all laws. Instead in the Peoples' Republics new codes merely supplanted those norms that were no longer appropriate. Some of the old judicial structures were left intact as long as it was made certain that they would respond to the imperatives of the new social and political order. Further differences between the U.S.S.R. and the Peoples' Republics have evolved from different methods in state planning. This is particularly true in Yugoslavia, where the leadership has made a number of original contributions to legal thought and practice in a socialist economy.

For all their differences the three legal families briefly described so far have one important trait in common. They all are thoroughly secularized; norms as well as procedures have shed all sacral characteristics. The "legal formalism" (to use Max Weber's term) [27] which pervades all of the Western legal families can serve a variety of regimes and ideological ends. Ethical and in some cases religious convictions may frequently enter the legal process in its various phases. But they do so through a seemingly rational and abstract process which filters beliefs through preestablished, rather than ad hoc, through generic rather than personalized concepts.

The Non-Western Legal Families   Thorough secularism is not characteristic of the systems belonging to the non-Western legal family. As previously stated the three legal families which are closely linked to European cultures have today spread to all continents. With a few exceptions such as Saudi Arabia and Afghanistan, all countries have felt the impact of Western legal traditions. But this does not preclude the survival of some indigenous legal cultures, notably in Asia and Africa.

In both the Islam and the Hindu civilizations, but also in some of the systems of black Africa and Madagascar, traditional legal cultures were largely facets of religious life. It is not easy to decide the question of

[27] See Weber, 1954, p. 219.

whether the frequently oral customs of black Africa can properly be considered as law.[28] With the beginning of the colonial period large sectors of African law were modeled either by legislative action or by administrative regulation on the various Western systems following the civil-law or the common-law traditions, that is, on those of France, Belgium, Portugal, or England. Traditional law and native courts were not so much attacked or made illegal as they were ignored. Independence has, on the whole, ushered in a more positive attitude towards traditional law and its underlying principles of solidarity to the group rather than to the individual. But there is clearly no intention on the part of the new regimes to reverse the trend towards the Westernization of legal rules or to abolish modern legal institutions.

In countries that came under the sway of Confucian thought, such as traditional China and Japan, ritual and not law was the foundation of the social order. Neither law-making nor the judicial process was looked upon as the normal means of maintaining or restoring harmony in these societies. In subsequent chapters references will be made occasionally to contrasting details of these cultures. But their legacy is too rich to be treated adequately within the limits of this book.[29]

From a comparative perspective the most fascinating aspect is the way in which non-Western cultures have accepted, rejected, or transformed Western systems. That Japan, since the beginning of the Meiji era in 1868, has most thoroughly westernized her law might not be surprising. In doing so she has been frankly eclectic, choosing from French, German, and lately Anglo-American law. Yet in the actual process of adjudication, of settling conflicts between individuals, the 2,000-year-old Confucian ways of thinking frequently outweigh Western ways.

In the modernizing Moslem countries codifications on the basis of either the French, German, or Swiss code have proceeded apace, while the Moslem Union Republics in the U.S.S.R. and some African countries have followed the socialist example. In close to thirty countries in which 400 million Moslems live the stage of economic modernization has determined the mixture of the modern and the traditional in legal relationships. Generally Moslem legal culture has always excelled in reconciling seeming immutability and flexibility. At least in some systems questions of personal status have remained in the traditional mold. By contrast the law of contracts is almost entirely Western-modern; but several of the codes admonish the judge to have recourse to the Koran if difficulties of interpretation should arise.

[28] David and Brierley, 1968, p. 462; also see pp. 461–85 for a succinct analysis of African legal development.

[29] For an excellent comparative treatment of the Oriental traditions and their contrast with Western law, see Bozeman, 1971.

In India the law of the Hindu community had long been stunted in its development by Moslem domination. After the British arrival three legal cultures existed in the subcontinent, with each exercising its separate jurisdiction. The British tried to further unification by introducing large parts of the English common law through comprehensive codifications, hence using techniques of the civil law. While official India now belongs to the common-law family, the legal system trying to bind together an enormous and far from homogeneous population under a fairly decentralized judicial system has been compared to that of the United States rather than to that of England.[30] But for the vast majority of Indians, especially those in rural regions, the traditional Hindu culture still provides the norms for legal relations in everyday life.

Subsequent chapters will occasionally comment on the quite extraordinary case of Communist China. The outside observer discovers much in its legal thought and practices which reminds him of Confucian traditions—including the fact that to speak of "legal" procedures might already be considered a misnomer by the Chinese. But the regime denies any such legacy and insists on fundamental differences. It also insists that fundamental differences exist between the Chinese and the systems that have aligned themselves with the Soviet Union. At least for the time being the Chinese legal culture may indeed lay claim to a category of its own.

[30] David and Brierley, 1968, p. 433.

THE SOURCES OF LAW

2

Sources of law are the materials out of which legal rules are fashioned once distinctively legal obligations have emerged in society. Customs based here on religions, there on secular traditions, decisions by judicial bodies or other notables, written rules, standards of justice, and, possibly, authoritative writings about the law furnish these materials. Singly or more frequently in combination these are the sources common to all legal orders: African tribal judges base their decisions on them as does the U.S. Supreme Court.[1] However, the relative importance given to these sources by the various legal families, or indeed by different members of the same family, varies strikingly. While in general cultural differences have been decisive for such preferences, historical situations, stability or upheaval, slow economic mutations, or a technological breakthrough may impose the use of one source rather than another. Throughout history each of these sources has had its ideological defenders who were inclined to see the virtues of wisdom and justice restricted to those sources that seemed to serve best their own interests and values.

CUSTOM AND JUDICIAL PRECEDENTS Custom is not only the oldest but also an ubiquitous source of law: it prescribes behavior that through continued observance has become "customary" and it announces sanctions for deviant behavior. What distinguishes mere habits from customary law is the coercive force that is gathered behind the latter. The proof that a rule has long been observed will benefit effective enforcement even though the "general immemorial custom of the realm" on which the English common law is theoretically based was never more than a fiction, and one not

[1] See Gluckman, 1955, pp. 15–24.

universally applied. Because its origins are frequently unknown and sometimes shrouded in mystery, custom will be praised by some as being embedded in popular faith rather than consciously created by an elite. But
to be able to rely on custom will also be helpful to that elite when the time
has come to formulate a legal rule. For to create legal norms out of a
vacuum requires too great an intellectual effort.[2] At least at an early stage
true custom will always be narrowly local and will remain parochial. Only
when local customs are fused and, in the process, transformed will they
remain functional and thereby avoid being swept away by other rules of
broader application. Usually the practice of custom will be hardened and
made more definite either by regular adjudication or by its incorporation
into legislation.

In England the King's itinerant judges amalgamated on their circuits
the widely differing local customs into a common custom. After a time, the
common law of the realm was used synonymously with customary law and
an increasingly influential bench and bar thus did their part not only in
creating a national legal culture but in welding together a nation. Although
it was stretched out over time and was continuously seeking its justification
in the past, the creation of a common law was in its effects as revolutionary
as comprehensive codification elsewhere. What was repeated again and
again, either by the members of the society or by the elite sitting in judgment of the acts of common men, was deemed good and beneficial.[3] In
this way a judge-made law was given the appearance of being intimately
tied to the people's habits, their wisdom, and their consent. The function
of the judiciary was to make customs concrete and explicit by applying
"legal reason" to the cases brought before them. Custom and court decisions
were and have remained singly or intertwined a primary, though not the
only, source of law in common-law systems.

The legitimation which the judges gave to their activity by building
their decisions on a seemingly uninterrupted sequence of cases could not
have been maintained if each situation coming before the courts had been
looked at afresh, on its own terms. Hence the binding force of *precedent,*
an obligation to subsume new decisions under the principles of previous
ones, was, at least in theory, a keystone to the viability of the common law.
The actual workings of this principle of *stare decisis* in various systems of
the common-law family and, on the other hand, the role which judicial
precedents are playing in code-law systems, will be discussed below
(Chapter 6).

The judges' obligation not to depart from precedent in the gradual
building of the common law protected them from arbitrary directives issued

---

[2] Paton, 1972, pp. 192f.

[3] See (also for the following) Bendix, forthcoming.

by the king. Behind this shield a judiciary, which in fact was closely tied to landowning interests, was able not only to protect its own power and status but also to appear as the people's defenders against executive power. English judges acquired thereby a prestige which their brethren on the European continent were found lacking when dissatisfaction with the executive led to upheavals.

Developing legal ideas from case to case was giving bench and bar a prominence which they were unwilling to lose to an active legislator. In early seventeenth century England, Chief Justice Coke spoke of statutes as "raging tyrants"; as late as the nineteenth century a Chief Justice in New Hampshire castigated the "devices of ignorance called codes." Such attitudes had, in spite of some legislative successes, defeated Bentham's attempts at large-scale codification; it is true that in England no systematic legal science had developed the categories which have assisted the efforts of most codifiers.[4] Hostility to legislation, coupled with an unbounded enthusiasm for the "common-law way of life," have not entirely died out among some of the legal elites on both sides of the Atlantic. They sometimes overlook that building the law by precedent works best as long as development proceeds in a steady flow without deep cleavages between the historical situations in which important cases are decided. The method which has a conservative bent because of its constant reference to the past, frequently fails when shattered social conditions are pressing for quick, well-defined regulation.[5]

To such a proposition the defenders of the common law have responded that drastic reform legislation has often resulted in statutes whose announced policies have proven unworkable yet which froze the announced rules for a prolonged time. Only the courts, they will argue, can bring facts into focus; their role in sifting and transforming interstitially unsuitable rules promises more satisfactory results.

In fact, and quite understandably, the American legal culture has not always stood as steadfastly as the English for the cause of the common law. In early colonial times the onrush of new problems, the dislike for the close ties between the common law and the feudal order, and also the lack of a sufficiently large corps of lawyers who would have been familiar with the substance of the common law, encouraged in Massachusetts and elsewhere some significant codifications. If in the end the country remained within the common-law culture, the common language and convenient compilations of the English law which became the vogue soon after American independence have undoubtedly facilitated communication. Probably most important was the fact that the number of lawyers increased rapidly and that they, like their British colleagues, came to see the law primarily in terms

---

[4] Weber, 1954, p. 341.

[5] Radbruch, 1936, pp. 531f.

of litigation. Where the common law of England proved insufficient for the needs of the communities in the New World, American judges did not hesitate to declare which customs of the settlers deserved to supplement the law.

Outside of common-law countries the survival of custom as a source of law is frequently regarded as an archaic legacy which will give way sooner or later to more modern ways of shaping the legal system of a nation. This is generally true, although everywhere, in developing as well as in developed countries, custom may find its way into the judicial decisions of completely codified systems. It has already been mentioned that the newly independent countries of Africa frequently pay respect to their traditional law which was largely customary. They seek to fuse its spirit and, if possible, some of its norms with the westernized systems which they have accepted as their own. But there are also modern and increasingly frequent uses of custom in some of the most highly industrialized societies. Where an over-centralized bureaucracy complicates the daily life and the interactions of citizens, the customs of "miniature legal systems" might meet the need for efficiency.

The customs of the trading communities within or beyond national borders have long been recognized, even without being codified, as binding rules of conduct; the same is often true in industrial relations. Modern customs as formulated somewhat unilaterally by corporation lawyers are also incorporated into the innumerable form contracts which have already been mentioned. The frequency and importance of the relationships which they create are tantamount to a return to custom as a significant source of law in the legal cultures of our times.

LEGISLATION AND CODIFICATION

Where customary law and the common law are building on human experiences of the past, legislation steps forward to announce how future behavior will be regulated. Where customary law never denies that it is the product of social forces, legislation has, among the various sources of law, the foremost claim to act as an independent variable which sets into motion societal and political change. Where the common law is the product of a legal elite which for all its cohesion operates in a decentralized manner, legislation is created and imposed from a center of decision-making by a sovereign whoever that sovereign may be: a despot, a prince, a politbureau, the bureaucracy, or a legislative assembly.

Although the legislative way has ultimately triumphed in many cultures as a predominant source of law, it is not exclusively modern, just as there were written constitutions before the modern age. While absent from primitive law, statutory enactments are well known in so-called archaic legal cultures. The laws of Moses, Lycurgus, and Draco, and the Roman Twelve Tables (451 B.C.), are all sources of written laws whose social meaning remains obscure. Yet the interpretations that have been offered are paradigms of much subsequent legislation in other settings: they have been regarded as either the expression of a plebeian revolt against the patricians or as the expression of popular conservatism fighting surreptitious reforms.[6] The canon law, the codified legal system of the Catholic Church, stated quite succinctly in the twelfth century the foremost function of legislation: "New ills demanded the discovery of new medicines."

In functional terms single statutes and comprehensive codes are not fundamentally different. Both of them either systematize and clarify existing norms, or they are a deliberate departure setting out to correct former practices. Of course the two objectives may be pursued at the same time, and frequently are. Codifications usually amount to a systematic and comprehensive compilation of norms; they seek to regulate a broad sector of relationships with the greatest possible economy, and this is usually attained by generalizing juristic concepts. Statutes deal with a single or a few subjects, however involved or many-sided. But when statutes are in need of amendment or of consolidation, the legislator might have to draft texts that resemble codification.

Today all systems, including those of common-law traditions, rely for much of their legal life on legislation. Most of the higher courts of the United States and of Great Britain as well deal far more with statutory law than with common-law rules. But in the same countries the reluctance to get involved in comprehensive codifications has not been overcome. California is generally regarded as "the leading code state" in the United States. Extensive codification of private law was undertaken there, not only because common-law traditions were thin, but also because it seemed necessary to end once and for all the lingering influence of Mexican law. But neither the text of the codes nor its application have been deemed as satisfactory as the working of the codes in civil-law countries. The same is true of some federal codes. In spite of outward appearances these codes do not express the same cultural reality as the European codes; judges are not compelled to find a basis for deciding a given case within the code but might and frequently will look to other sources.[7]

The codifications that, beginning with the early nineteenth century, swept Europe from the Atlantic to the Urals, were in fact due to a political constellation quite different from that of England and its colonies. Where through the royal judges the common law had been the great, if gradual, unifier of diversified customs, the French Revolution, as later the newly

---

[6] Ehrenzweig, 1971, p. 123.

[7] Merryman, 1969, p. 33.

founded German Reich, was faced by the disorderly universe of multiple customary or territorial laws. Modest attempts by the French monarchs to unify the existing law were defeated by the regional *parlements*. These were in fact judicial bodies which were holding onto a law that was serving the interests of feudal seigneurs and local notables. The resulting chaos and injustice identified the judiciary with the worst aspects of the regime which the revolution set out to overturn.[8]

"You want good laws?" Voltaire had exclaimed. "Burn yours and make new ones!" Such optimistic faith in the benefits of novelty paired with a positivistic belief that the legal order was all that was needed to effect change conformed to the spirit of the enlightment; it also expressed the mood of all major codifications. Politically colorless in appearance they have served various regimes but have always been undertaken when the elites in a society reach a consensus that it is useful to restructure norms and institutions.

The codes initiated by Napoleon embodied the values and interests of the new bourgeois order at the beginnings of industrialization. They protected the property owner, the employer, and the creditor, and strengthened the position of the father and husband. The Third Estate, trusting the force of reason, also sought emancipation from the advice of the judicial caste which it suspected. Hence the style of the new codes was to be "as simple as the bible," self-sufficient, and presumably not in need of learned interpretation. Napoleon enjoined the legal profession from publishing any commentary on the codes; the emperor Justinian had made a similar, and similarly futile, attempt to prove that the codification he had undertaken was complete and definitive.

In France, the Civil Code has outlived more than a dozen political constitutions. Compared to their total, the number of articles that have undergone significant change is not large. But codes presumably based on human reason could also be presented as an instrument of beneficial liberation from social and political fetters beyond national borders. The codes that were introduced in the wake of Napoleon's conquests have, in most cases, survived the fall of the emperor. When the German philosopher Hegel described Napoleon as the "*Weltgeist* on horseback," he thought above all of his legal reform work.

The German Civil Code of 1900, the *Bürgerliche Gesetzbuch*, had, like its French equivalent, the task of unifying a multitude of legal systems and by doing so to support a monolithic nation-state.[9] But beyond these intentions, style and even some of the functions were different from the

---

[8] Tocqueville (1856), 1955, pp. 95–100.

[9] Merryman, 1969, p. 33. *Bürgerlich* means literally bourgeois. The German Civil Code had been preceded by a comprehensive codification of the criminal law.

French Code. The new German Reich was not the issue of a revolution. Instead of civil servants following the directives of an usurper, German professors tried to conserve and to codify the principles that emerged from their historical study of existing law which had also been influenced profoundly by the reception of Roman law. They did not believe that one should rid the system of lawyers; instead their text was designed so that it would need professional and learned interpretation by the judiciary for its application to concrete cases (for details, see below, Chapter 6). The lag in time also made a difference. Instead of the unbridled individualism of the French code, a more cautious and distinctly paternalistic bent expressed the temper of the German middle classes won over by Bismarck's successes and installed in a society in which modern and traditional values intermingled. Because of such characteristics the German code, rather than the older French code, proved a ready import for rapidly industrializing countries such as Japan.

After the Soviet Union had abandoned its design for sending all law to the ash cans of history it entered an age of wholesale legislation and codification. All reference to the laws and judicial decisions of czarist Russia remained forbidden. But every important stage of political and economic development was accompanied by successive waves of statutory enactments on either the federal or the Union Republic level. After the Second World War the same process occurred in the Soviet orbit countries. Legislation alone became and has remained the admitted source for law. The positivistic creed, which was first practiced in revolutionary France and which maintains that the legislative texts reveal all legal relations without any need for interpretation, has never been preached as steadfastly as in the Communist countries:

> It is codification and codification alone [wrote a Hungarian jurist in 1960 and 1961] that can insure, in the course of the transformation of society, the progressive role of the people's democratic law as a new socialist law. . . .
>   . . . In socialist law the purpose of legislation is not to camouflage the will of the ruling class. It follows that the idea and the role of legislative interpretation are necessarily limited, since the will of the legislator does not allow, either at the time of promulgation or later on, that the substance of the legal rules be changed under the pretext of interpretation. . . . In bourgeois law, the judge has become the pivot of the legal system. Socialist evolution has not made this error. Any remedial "interpretation" is contrary to the principles of Marxism-Lenism.[10]

The "bourgeois" Jeremy Bentham, whose principles were discussed in the preceding chapter, would have subscribed to many of these propositions.

[10] I. Szabo, quoted here from David and Brierley, 1968, pp. 246f.

Engaged as they are in thorough political and socioeconomic renovation, all of the developing countries, whatever the nature of their regimes, have resorted to massive legislation and codification. The degree to which their new codes have either incorporated or eliminated earlier customary law or colonial legislation has varied from country to country. Other, and often substantial, differences have resulted from varied traditional legal cultures. In the Arab countries the Islamic concept that the sovereign power, whether it be represented by a monarch or a parliamentary body, is not the master but the servant of the law, seemingly prevented the exercise of legislative powers. But since it has always been admitted that the civil authorities could exercise sweeping police powers for the purpose of maintaining public order, legislation and codifications were introduced, at first haltingly, but of late in an increasing number of countries. How much these compilations reflect Western influences or cling to basic concepts of Moslem law, depends on the general outlook of the regime.[11]

In China the way to codification and legislation was opened with the revolution of 1911. During the first decades of the Chinese Republic the badge of Westernization was a heavy legislative output whose outward appearances seemed to put the country into the Romano-Germanic family of legal systems. But traditional concepts of law (to be discussed below, Chapter 3) and the lack of a sufficiently large number of jurists left much of the not-so-legal culture untouched. During their first decade in power the Chinese Communists followed the Soviet example of legislating change. Since then they have moved away from written law as a means of social control. Concurrently the emphasis which the Soviet Union and the Peoples' Democracies have placed on legislation and on codified legal procedures was denounced by the Chinese leaders as yet another example of Moscow's commitment to "theories of bourgeois jurisprudence."[12]

As will be shown below (Chapter 6), law-making and policy determination through the judicial process have not lost their importance. But in all countries, highly industrialized as well as those in the process of development, "legislation is the most obvious way of bringing political will to bear for the purpose of effecting social change through law."[13] Most of the time this is due to social and technological imperatives rather than to ingrained legal traditions. New concerns, such as the development or the preservation of natural and human resources, the consequences of increased mobility, the population explosion, and pollution, call not only for new legal rules but also

---

[11] David and Brierley, 1968, pp. 399 and 404ff.

[12] Hazard, 1969, pp. 96ff.

[13] Selznick, 1968, p. 56.

for the creation of the appropriate agencies to administer the new legislation. "Law is rather produced like industrial consumer goods, in such quantities that no one can survey the process." [14]

Hence, in order to bring some order out of chaos, periodic needs arise for either new codifications or, at least, comprehensive compilations of existing laws. While in the end legislatures will have to enact the proposed texts, be they mere compilations or reforms, parliaments in most countries are not particularly interested in passing on long bills which are devoid of immediate political interest.[15] The work must be prepared for them by appropriate committees of legal experts. In the United States unofficial but prestigious bodies such as the American Law Institute, supported by all branches of the legal profession, have put together a series of Restatements that are very similar to the extensive codifications in civil-law countries. As is nearly always the case, the process of clarification also involves changes of existing law. In some countries where the judges are empowered as a body to make suggestions for the reform of the law, not many changes have been forthcoming from this source. However, in England, in several Commonwealth countries, in France, and in the Soviet Union, the government itself has established law commissions charged with reviewing entire fields of law with a view toward making recommendations for systematization or overhauling.

While the commissions are composed of legal practitioners, they endeavor to receive suggestions from the outside. The Soviet government reported that in the post-Stalinist era, tens of thousands of people, jurists and nonjurists alike, were drawn into the process of law reforms which were then submitted to the appropriate Soviets. In Canada, and especially in the Province of Quebec, efforts at enlisting citizens in the work of a Law Reform Commission have met with only moderate success. There are few communications from the general public. Proposals that have been made originate usually with organized pressure groups. Moreover in Canada, as elsewhere, parliament is free to reject the proposals made by the Commission although it must consider them. But at any rate, this is a far cry from Napoleon dictating—as the legend goes—entire sections of the codes to his appointees, or the German law professors pondering over their treatises.

EQUITY   The problem of how to mitigate the possible harshness and iniquity of established norms by considerations of justice has preoccupied legal thinking and practice at least since Aristotle. In systems where adjudication is characterized by what Max Weber has called "khadi justice,"

[14] Stone, 1966, p. 156.
[15] Paton, 1972, p. 261, and Friedmann, 1967, pp. 511ff.

such tension need not arise since rulings are not determined by a formally rational law, but instead are oriented on ethical, religious, or political postulates which can make due allowance for what appears equitable.[16] But wherever the judicial process has been rationalized the question of whether law alone is a sufficient source for the satisfactory settlement of conflicts cannot always be eluded.

In England equity developed as a separate source of law because of special historical circumstances. In an essentially static feudal society the common law had well served the interests of landed property. Bench and bar, closely allied with such interests, also found intellectual satisfaction in elaborating a legal system which in losing its earlier flexibility became ever more technical.[17] Claims which could not be fitted into established writs were denied, so that in an increasing number of cases no solution could be found. Redress was sought and found by a direct appeal to the king from the fourteenth century onwards. The king's chancellor, who was also his confessor, decided on the basis of the "equity of the case," and this allowed for fast remedies and altogether provided at least a modicum of equal treatment to parties that were unequal in status and resources. But what at first had been an exceptional recourse became institutionalized. A special system of equity courts developed which gave to the legal culture of the country a kind of "legal polytheism" akin to concepts of political pluralism. A number of legal institutions (such as the "trust") unknown to other systems grew out of equity procedures. Also important was the fact that the possibility of being either a common lawyer or an equity lawyer created sharp differences in the legal profession itself.

It cannot be explained here how the common law eventually escaped the danger of being eliminated by the equitable jurisdiction of the chancery. For a while conflicts raged and then abated, until at the end of the nineteenth century the formal distinction between the two kinds of courts was abolished in England as it had been earlier in the United States. But if the same courts are now privileged to apply the norms of the common law as well as of equity, the latter need no longer be considered as a formal source of law. Yet equitable considerations and remedies have not been banned from judicial decisions. The situation has been assimilated to what has always been a possibility in civil-law systems. Judges may try to mitigate injustices, which would result from too rigid an application of formal rules, by considerations of "natural justice." Some modern codes actually direct

---

[16] See Weber (1922), 1954, p. 213. This is actually not an adequate description of the way in which the khadis, the lower Moslem magistrates, arrived at their decisions. It represents, however, a widely prevalent prerational form of lawfinding.

[17] See Bendix, forthcoming, and David and Brierley, 1968, pp. 287ff.

them, albeit in a limited number of cases, to proceed in such a way. The Federal Civil Code of Mexico (1928), as well as a number of the civil codes of the Mexican states, dispenses judges from applying the general rule that ignorance of the law does not protect against the consequences of such ignorance, if, in view of the parties' social condition, the application of the rule would amount to an injustice. Where such practices prevail, it is the individual decision which must resolve the possible tension between the norms of positive law and the commands of justice.

Although all Western systems have remained sensitive to this dualism, a system of revealed law, such as the traditional Moslem law, is bound to deny it. For to invoke against the law higher principles of "natural reason" would destroy the unity of the legal order.

SUBSIDIARY SOURCES   Legal writings, the treatises and commentaries by legal scholars, were at one time regarded as an important source of law in the systems belonging to the Romano-Germanic family. The predominant role which continental universities played in the education of lawyers during the middle ages and early modern times, and the need to translate and explain the Roman law and thereby create a national legal terminology, were among the reasons why European jurists paid close attention to *la doctrine*. Its impact was even greater because scholars often occupied judicial offices and judges held teaching assignments in the universities. Later the reliance of legislators on scholarly advice made it useful for judges to be familiar with the scholars' concepts.

The increase of legislative activities was bound to diminish the role of legal writings as an independent source of law. However, the thoroughly modern Swiss Civil Code of 1907 directs the judge, when he finds a gap in the law, to act as if he were the legislator, "guided by approved legal doctrine and judicial tradition." Hence it puts legal writings on an equal footing with precedents. The Italian Civil Code of 1942 is even more sweeping in its recommendations to use subsidiary sources. Whenever the judge has exhausted other methods of law-finding he should decide "according to the general principles of the jurisprudential organization of the state." This also may include reference to legal writings, since in all Latin countries the prestige of the law professors remains considerable. Especially in Latin America *la doctrine* is highly, and frequently dogmatically, developed, but there is controversy over the extent to which it actually influences legal decisions and culture.[18]

In traditional Moslem law the ijmā, the unanimous agreement of legal scholars, was considered one of the main sources of law besides the Koran

[18] David and Brierley, 1968.

and the Sunna (the latter is a record of collected traditions). The modernization and extensive codification of Moslem law have not driven out entirely
either custom or the other traditional sources which under certain circumstances are still regarded as more important than the term "subsidiary"
suggests.

In Anglo-American law reliance on sources other than the common
law, judicial precedent, and legislation is hardly acknowledged. The fact
that in the common-law countries legal scholarship, for all its wealth and
originality, is respected but not regarded as a source of law might be termed
an intellectual injustice. For legal writings do play a considerable role in
argument before the courts and in the rulings of at least the higher courts.
If in this respect a difference between civil-law and common-law countries
survives, it must be explained by a seemingly different outlook on the
nature of legal skills. Whether the legal culture regards such skills as the
expression of a craft or an art, or as the product of the scientific mind, will
lead to divergent conclusions concerning the value of scholarship for justice
in action. This has consequences for the legal training and the self-image of
the legal elites to be discussed below (see Chapter 4).

THE ENDS OF LAW

OF

LAW

3

"Everywhere law begins," a caustic American observer has stated, "when somebody is doing something which somebody else doesn't like." It follows that the ends of the law are, if not the elimination, at least the control of the disturbance caused by one side and resented by the other side. On either or both sides one may of course find individuals as well as corporate bodies, private or public. And the parties invoking "the law" will always be found to develop mutually inconsistent claims to a given resource.[1]

In countries in which the law is recognized as an important carrier of shared values and, simultaneously, as an agent of social control, the question arises, which values will it mobilize in order to control the trespass that has been complained of? Simplistic answers abound. "Apply the law and you will have order," is the solution for the "strict constructionists" who are to be found in many countries. They are contradicted by those for whom the dictates of "justice" will distribute "to each his due." Categoric answers such as these do not acknowledge the tension between conflicting values and multiple functions of the law, and will therefore be unable to explain why in different cultural settings and historical situations the law might be effective or might fail.

Which then are the values potentially alive in all law, but always prone to enter into conflict? The commands of justice require that equals and equal situations be treated equally. But who is to judge what is equal and what is unequal? Should such judgment separate individuals from their status and social relationships as is done in principle though not in practice in most western but not in all societies? And even after equalities and inequalities have been stated how are they to be treated in concrete decisions? Difficulties in answering these questions arise from the fact that justice

[1] Abel, 1974, p. 227.

represents only one side of the law, the formal side.[2] It forbids, in the words of Anatole France, the millionaire and the pauper alike to sleep under bridges and to steal stale bread. Justice becomes concrete only when it is recognized that utility also serves the ends of law. Society, and in modern times the state, will determine what is to be considered useful, and will establish priorities accordingly. The law, from whatever source it may derive, will then be relied upon to transform public policies into norms for the behavior of citizens and officials alike.

Standards of utility cannot help but pervade the law with political and often ideological content; they add flexibility and relativity to the formal and abstract dimension of justice. Yet an unbridled relativity of values, constantly changing priorities, would not satisfy the requirements of a legal order. To fulfill the ends of law its rules and procedures must also be as stable as possible. As John Dewey has noted:

> Men need to know the legal consequences which society through the courts will attach to their specific transactions, the liabilities they are assuming, the fruits they may count upon for a given course of action.[3]

If law were unable to provide for stability and a modicum of certainty, it would generate discord rather than prevent it. This is why Justice Brandeis, well known for his sense of justice and his concern for social utility, could once say: "It is usually more important that a rule of law be settled than that it be settled right."

If the triad of justice, utility, and security describes adequately the near-universal ends of law, it also must be understood that the relationship among the three values of law is relative and may give rise to considerable tensions. How they will be resolved or mitigated, how far utility should prevail over justice, or security over utility, each political system must decide.[4] Max Weber stated this as a general proposition: "all [authorities] are confronted by the inevitable conflict between an abstract formalism of legal certainty and their desire to realize substantive goals." Writing at the same time as his German colleague, the American legal scholar Dean Pound perceived a "continual movement in legal history back and forth between justice without law, as it were, and justice according to law." [5]

---

[2] What follows was suggested in his life work by G. Radbruch, one of the foremost German legal philosophers; see Radbruch, 1950, p. 50 and the entire Chapter 7 entitled "The Purpose of Law."

[3] Dewey, 1924, p. 24.

[4] Friedmann, 1967, p. 193.

[5] Both Weber and Pound are quoted here from Abel, 1974, p. 303.

When in dynamic societies the desire for change is to be translated into legal norms, the unavoidable formality of law and, frequently, difficulties in enforcing the new rules will act as a hedge against the impetuousness of the reform-mongers. Elsewhere changes might be deliberately slow and discontinuous; then a successful appeal to justice can modify, possibly through the judicial process, legal relationships that no longer correspond to the true needs of the society.

Because law is both an instrument of change and an object of such changes as have occurred in society, the ends of law will seldom be identified for long with a single value. At different times the U.S. Supreme Court has developed different strains in the American political and legal culture. Until well into our century, and even while a major depression ravaged the economy, it protected those who managed the laissez-faire economy and their expectations of secure enjoyment of privileges. In contrast the postwar court by setting increasingly high standards of equality has developed an egalitarian emphasis. Everywhere the law can either introduce new norms into a culture or reinforce and rehabilitate old ones by reordering priorities.[6]

RIGHTS AND DUTIES All Western legal systems, including those of the socialist countries, recognize that the individual is entitled to certain rights which the legal order promises to safeguard. Corresponding obligations will at the very least forbid the interference with other peoples' rights, but might also include a number of positive duties. The scope and nature of both rights and duties determine the characteristics of any polity. Rights and duties may be formulated in the language of natural law, or they may be described in utilitarian fashion. But they will always furnish to the Western systems the chapter headings for their codes or the categories informing their judicial decisions.

For contrasting language the French Declaration of the Rights of Man of 1789 (explicitly referred to as being still valid in the Fifth French Republic) can be compared with the Fundamental Principles of Civil Law that the U.S.S.R. issued in 1961 (and which are restated in the new civil codes of the orbit countries). The former promised that the enjoyment of natural rights

> limits only those [rights] that assure other members of the society enjoyment of these same rights; such limits may be determined only by law. . . . What is not forbidden by law may not be prevented and no one may be compelled to do what it does not prescribe.

---

[6] See Grossman and Sarat, 1971, p. 199.

.

The Soviet Union stated:

Civil rights are protected by law, except in instances when they are exercised in a manner inconsistent with their purpose in a socialist society in the period of the building of communism. In exercising their rights and performing their obligations, citizens and organizations must observe the law, and must respect the rules of socialist communal living and the moral principles of a society which is building communism.

The application of these principles (and, frequently their spectacular nonapplication) has produced drastically different results in the political systems for which they were formulated. What the declarations have in common is not only the recognition of individual rights but also the acknowledgement that such rights may be limited in certain prescribed forms usually referred to as the "rule of law" (to be discussed later in this chapter). Established as well as newly claimed rights will be asserted successfully when they are in accordance with the moral convictions of the community or, more accurately, of the legal elite that speaks and decides for the community. The assertion of new rights, however "just" in the eyes of many, or of new duties, might always be harmful to the stability of the system. The legal order will then have to determine which balance to strike and whether to grant or to deny the claim made by either public authorities, or a group, or an individual.

We have become accustomed to the fact that in the modern welfare state new demands translated into new legislation will almost invariably tend to regulate and thereby limit private rights or that they will formulate new duties incumbent upon individuals. But the long uphill fight waged in the United States to establish a previously unrecognized "right to be left alone" furnishes an example of extending private rights into new spheres. At the end of the last century a prominent Bostonian family became irritated with gossipy but never libelous newspaper columns reporting on the details of its social life. Neither the common law nor legislation had recognized a right to privacy, and indeed such a claim had to be weighed against the right of the public to know what was or might become its business. A searching article by respected lawyers in the *Harvard Law Review* established the foundations for the new right which little by little made its way into court decisions until it was confirmed, fairly recently, in a ringing declaration by the Supreme Court. The occasion was a decision that invalidated a Connecticut statute which made it a crime to sell contraceptives or to give advice on their use to married couples.[7]

---

[7] See Warren and Brandeis, 1890, pp. 193ff., and Griswold v. Connecticut, 381 U.S. 479ff. (1965).

A similar attempt to establish a new right was made by the postwar Constitution for West Germany, the Basic Law of 1949. It admonished all public authorities to protect a "right to the free development of one's personality." So far there has not been a substantiation or implementation of this sweeping right which, after the nightmare of totalitarianism, was to serve as the symbol for a new legal order and for a new culture as well.

The position that different systems have taken with regard to the problem of the "good Samaritan" provides illustrations for the possibility of establishing new legal duties. Socialist countries have wavered on the question of whether a "duty to rescue" exists and whether an individual failing to perform such a duty would incur criminal sanctions or merely be liable for damages to a person in distress whom he has refused to assist. Civil-law countries—France, Portugal, and Austria among them—have come to recognize such a duty and have attached legal consequences to its neglect.[8] Elsewhere, for example in the United States, the most flagrant refusal to help another human being in distress might expose one to moral condemnations but not to legal sanctions of any kind. A comparison of legislative attitudes towards this problem suggests that here differences in legal culture are not the main determinants, but that countries with a significant rural population are more inclined to recognize a legal duty to help than are urbanized societies.

What has been exemplified in regard to some specific situations is quite generally true: economic and social developments will shape and, if necessary, redefine legal rights and duties and by doing so will overcome earlier differences rooted in traditions. Since all law is wedded to procedures, technical differences in asserting rights might survive for a time. But in spite of different starting points the common-law and the civil-law systems have constantly come closer to each other, since they both serve the needs of highly developed industrial countries. Differing ideologies might keep the legal solutions of the socialist countries in many respects apart from those of the two other main families. But with regard to relationships that are little affected by ideological differences the gap is also narrowing. What follows seeks to demonstrate this proposition for some important fields of legal life.

In modern times the law of contract (developed first in the late Roman law) has become the basic mechanism of legal development, for it deals with nothing less than the individual as a source of law.[9] The French Civil Code gave the most classical definition of this fact when it stated: "Con-

---

[8] See the comparative discussion in Hazard, 1969, pp. 412–15.

[9] Seagle, 1941, p. 253 and the entire Chapter 7, entitled "The Omnipotence of Contract."

tracts legally entered into . . . have the effect of laws on those who have formed them." At the outset there were some significant differences between the continental European and the English views on the validity of an agreement. The more practical and, in this case, sceptical English views distrusted contracts where something seemed to be given for nothing and adjudged them nil for lack of a "consideration." But little by little the cosmopolitan influence of commercial and maritime law has assimilated common-law and civil-law practices. At least prior to the First World War all private agreements were enforceable unless very strong reasons to the contrary, usually founded on an outrage to morality, were proven. With the greater impact of social consciousness and concern for the protection of the weaker parties to a bargain, legislation has almost everywhere put limits on the freedom to establish rights and duties by contract. An explicit provision of a recent Swedish statute entitles the courts to disregard or modify contractual obligations where one of the parties is found to be in a position of social or economic dependence.[10] A similarly creative role is now incumbent upon the British courts which are entitled to decide whether a testator has made a "reasonable" provision for his dependents. Where this is not the case a last will might be altered. Even at the apex of individualism most continental codes had stated which portions of an estate a testator could not remove from members of his immediate family.

In the Canadian province of Quebec, that continuing point of encounter between civil-law and common-law cultures, differences between the two systems can still be observed with regard to rights and duties which evolve from family and other intimate personal relationships. Because in these fields law is a means of expressing ethical and cultural self-determination, Quebec law has remained wedded to certain concepts of the Roman Catholic Church. In comparison, corresponding provisions derived from the common law express rather the values of a commercially minded trading community which puts a high priority on the mobility of labor and of population. Between these two models of legal life there has been little interaction or interchange and little inclination to develop a jurisprudence blending them.[11] Yet it must not be forgotten that only a relatively small sector of legal relationships is involved. Moreover the now ascending generation of Quebec lawyers is far less tradition-bound than their elders; hence changes also might be expected in this field.

Most present-day legal systems have sought to control the manifestations of an unbridled individualism by developing, either through court decisions or by legislation, a concept described widely, if unelegantly, as an

[10] Schmidt and Strömholm, 1964, p. 19.

[11] McWhinney, 1974, passim.

"abuse of rights." [12] It amounts to saying that a right, even when lawfully acquired, cannot be exercised for an end foreign to that for which it was given. In socialist countries no right will be enforced which is exercised in a manner "violating the principles of communal living." An essentially similar principle prevails in Western countries when they frown on the erection of spite fences, on unfair competition, or quite generally on the exercise of a right which has no other purpose than to harm some other person. However, a difference might subsist: at least in common-law countries the abuser loses the protection of the law only when he lacks good faith; in Communist countries the standards of society are made to prevail quite independently of the subjective disposition of the individuals. [13]

But to conclude that because of a more pronounced individualism the common law has recognized limitations on the use of rights more slowly than civil-law countries seems hardly warranted, once one looks not at procedural technicalities but at the results produced in life.

Legislative inroads on private property rights are a phenomenon common to all modern societies. Nonsocialist countries do not accept the distinction between ownership as a means of enjoyment of some basic needs and those aspects of property which convey power through the control of the means of production. While in socialist countries only the former is left in private hands, the legal systems of Western democracies provide far broader protection. Yet the bundle of rights identified with ownership of whatever kind (land, shares, firms, inventions, expectations) has lost much of the absoluteness it once laid claim to.

The notion of "propriété" in the French code of 1804 gave more absolute rights than did the notion of "ownership" in English and American law. Notwithstanding the existence of large French state monopolies, the civil law, which derived its property concepts from the Roman law, was geared to the needs of a country of small farms and small firms. Yet it did not know how to prevent by legal means the scattering of farm land among the owner's children. By comparison English property law has at all times appeared more functional: it recognized different degrees of control, not all of them absolute, and different forms of conveyance, some of them derived from feudal institutions but adaptable to a variety of modern needs.

On the continent the changeover from absolute property rights to a greater (if often still insufficient) emphasis on the duties of ownership was prepared by legal scholars motivated by different intellectual traditions. In France and in other Catholic countries the social philosophy of the church had an impact on legislation and court decisions in spite of the

---

[12] Paton, 1972, p. 474, quoting fairly concordant provisions from the German, a Chinese, the Soviet, and the Polish Civil Code.

[13] Hazard, 1969, p. 83.

separation of church and state. In Germany some romantic notions that were derived from village communities and medieval guilds were used to give to the exercise of property rights a less individualistic stance. But eventually the modern corporation with its typical separation of ownership and actual control has brought about a fundamental change not only in economic but also in legal relationships.[14] Legislation regulating corporations has become notably more uniform throughout the world. How to control by legal means the large corporations' power over natural and human resources is a problem which each regime must solve in accordance with its general outlook on the role of government in the economy.

In socialist countries and in the nationalized sectors of the economy in Western democracies such power is administered rather than controlled from the outside. Where in socialist countries property has remained in private hands, rules governing the rights and duties flowing from property and contracts are analogous to those recognized by modern civil and common law. As a matter of fact law suits involving these relationships hold a predominant place on the dockets of all Soviet courts. However, this does not give an accurate picture of the true importance of such suits. They may mean a great deal to the parties involved, but for the structure of the society at large they remain fairly insignificant.

The neglect of a "duty to care" exposes one in most legal cultures to tort claims. The tortfeasor is expected to make "whole" what his action or nonaction has destroyed or endangered. Where wrongful behavior has also disturbed the public order the legal system will pursue the trespasser for crime. The determination of what is considered as tort and as crime and which legal consequences are attached to both will always be closely tied to the moral standards and cultural values of a society. In addition the demands arising from technological change will affect the extent of duties and of sanctions.

The traditional civil and common law assessed damages only when there was proof that the tortfeasor's behavior involved fault, that is, some kind of guilt. In English law the moral element in tort law was particularly strong, even though not only intentional but possibly also negligent behavior was adjudged as morally wrong. The French code stated specifically that reparation was due only where there was "fault" on the part of him who had caused the damage. In a society where dangers and possible harms to persons and to material as well as immaterial interests have increased dramatically, the burden of proving the defendant's guilt was clearly too heavy. To insist on it would leave many harms without repair.[15]

---

[14] Berle and Means, 1932, remains a seminal treatise on this problem.

[15] This was for Holmes, later a Supreme Court Justice, the reason for a violent polemic against the prevailing views of the common law; see Holmes, 1881, esp. pp. 161–63.

When compensation became the main concern, because society was above all interested in restoring an equilibrium that had been disturbed, the search for guilt was deemphasized. An ever-widening field of potentially harmful activities was held to give rise to "strict" liability; damages were awarded when an injury had occurred even though no one might have been at fault. Different legal systems traveled separate ways to arrive at near-identical results. In order to bring code provisions in line with the requirements of modern society, French courts had to innovate in the same way common-law judges have developed the law. By broadly interpreting the spirit of the code and by building precedent upon precedent, they were able to award damages in spite of the wording of the code until new legislation became available.

If the modern law of torts seeks to provide insurance against a wide array of harms, insurance companies are in fact assuming the reparation of the damages that have occurred. In countries with comprehensive systems of social security the risk of living in a dangerous society is shared by the entire society. Where car drivers, property owners, and other categories are covered by voluntary or compulsory insurance, a substantial segment of the interested population contributes to the burden. Such practices have spread to all industrialized countries without regard for their legal traditions or for the different standards of care they might once have held.

When it comes to the assesment of damages two seemingly contradictory trends have emerged. Where in civil suits juries or other lay judges share in the verdict (see Chapter 5) they might regard grossly negligent or malevolent behavior as being also grossly immoral. Therefore they wish to inflict a punishment on the defendant by assessing high damages, possibly without regard for the actual harm done. At one time, moral, punitive, or exemplary damages were hardly recognized outside the common law. Now other systems also proceed in similar fashion and frequently in a way that obscures the division between liability for tort and for crime. On the other hand a verdict which wishes to compensate for injury in realistic fashion would want to take into account the financial position of both parties to a damage suit. An article of the civil code of the Soviet Union encourages such manifestations of "distributive justice" when it states: "In fixing damages the court must in all cases take into consideration the wealth of the injured person and the wealth of the party who caused the injury."

Although no such principle is stated in American law, the bias of juries frequently brings about analogous results, especially when it is known that ultimate financial responsibility will be born by a solvent insurance company. This, however, has had other, partly unforseen, consequences: namely, the contractual elimination of juries from civil cases and the settlement of damage claims out of court.

Compared to tort, crime is considered by society as sufficiently serious a disturbance to elicit the sterner sanction that is punishment. (In some cases the same act might give rise to both a damage suit by the injured party and to criminal prosecution.) The frequently slow transition from a legal order which entrusts the injured with sanctioning objectionable behavior to a system which recognizes a public interest in punishment, and eventually the state's monopoly for it, is a fascinating chapter in legal history. At different times and in different ways all legal cultures have turned this corner on their march towards modernization. In many primitive and archaic systems vengeance and blood feud were considered appropriate means of prosecuting a wrongdoer. Even at a late stage the Moslem law regarded the prosecution of a murderer as the prerogative of the victim's family; the strength of a custom of justified vendetta still surfaces in jury trials in Corsica and Sicily.

At all times the problem of criminal law, described by an American philosopher as "one of the most disheartening ones that face modern civilization," [16] has involved fundamental human beliefs and instincts. Unavoidably it also continues to arouse passionate disagreements even in communities characterized otherwise by a broad cultural consensus. The controversies about capital punishment in many countries are only a symptom of such basic disagreements. What follows singles out some problems of criminal liability for comparative consideration. Here too rights and duties are at stake: while the individual living in a community has the duty not to disturb the public order as defined by criminal law, he also has the right to claim that punishment be meted out according to established rules.

Nulla poena sine lege is an old maxim to which many legal systems have paid at least lip service and which has been embodied in many criminal codes as well as in bills of constitutional rights. It means above all that an offender should not be punished for any action without a clear and definite legal basis; it ought to exclude the possibility of giving retroactive effect to a criminal statute.

In totalitarian countries such safeguards are explicitly denied. A Nazi law of 1935 empowered the courts to punish according to "fundamental concepts of a penal law and of sound popular feelings." Ten years earlier the Penal Code of the Russian Soviet Federated Socialist Republic (RSFSR) had defined as crime "any socially dangerous act or commission which threatens the foundations of the Soviet political structure." Such provisions exposed the defendant to ad hoc punishment without the possibility of knowing in advance which actions might be considered criminal. The same situation prevailed as long as Soviet judges were invited by the legislator to convict "by analogy" using articles of the criminal code "most closely ap-

[16] M. Cohen, 1940, p. 987.

proximating, in gravity and in kind, to the crimes actually committed." Solzhenitsyn's report on close to forty years of Soviet practice reveals the full extent of human misery which results from such a "flexibility" of the criminal law.[17] As with the case of Nazi Germany one must conclude that where there is unlimited discretion one can no longer discern a system of law. In this sense the "law of totalitarianism" is a contradiction in terms.[18]

Even in countries respecting the maxim of *nulla poena sine lege* guarantees against discretionary punishment have not always been watertight. The most comprehensively codified criminal law can never foresee nor describe in detail the kind of behavior that will fall under the purview of the law. Like all legislation a penal statute can be construed narrowly or liberally. Which method is chosen is always a policy choice that will depend not only on the courts preference but on the general outlook on crime and punishment prevailing at a particular historical moment in a particular society.

The reliance of the common law on precedents which frequently invite different interpretations has often made the situation of defendants quite precarious. More generally the vigor of the common law in protecting the public order against all disturbances and its insistence on enforcing morals by means of the criminal law have permitted the survival of the so-called common-law crimes. As late as 1962 the British House of Lords maintained in a celebrated case dealing with an illustrated prospectus of available call girls that there existed in common law an offense of conspiracy to "corrupt public morals." [19] It is true that the decision was severely criticized as a blow to the principle of the specificity of criminal law. In more than one-third of the American states, and in Canada since its new criminal code of 1954, common-law offenses are no longer indictable except when they have been incorporated into statutory enactments. Most of the African states that follow common-law traditions have taken a similar attitude and have frequently expressed their aversion to common-law offenses in their constitutions.

In post-Stalin Russia the Fundamental Principles of Criminal Law of 1958 specifically adhered to the principle of *nulla poena* when it defined a crime as a "socially dangerous act *provided by law*" and thereby abolished punishment by analogy. In the socialist regimes of Eastern Europe jurists had always been uncomfortable about too flexible an application of criminal statutes, while in Cuba revolutionary tribunals still deal with "enemies" on an ad hoc basis.[20]

---

[17] Solzhenitsyn, 1974.

[18] Neumann, 1942, pp. 447ff.

[19] Shaw v. Director of Public Prosecutions (1962), A.C. 220; on the problem of the "enforcement of morals" see also Devlin, 1965.

[20] Hazard, 1969, p. 526.

Yet in all socialist countries a still-existing category of "crimes against the state" remains broad enough to prosecute many kinds of political dissent. But trials dispensing "political justice" have been known in almost all legal systems (for further discussion see below, Chapter 7).

As in the field of torts apparently contradictory trends are transforming principles of traditional criminal law in many modern systems. An increasing proportion of modern criminal legislation in the areas of public welfare, transport, public health, and industrial safety provides for punishment without reference to subjective guilt. The penalty will usually only be a fine and involves no moral stigma. Here criminal courts (or administrative tribunals) are used to serve the ends of social regulation, and even though punishment is inflicted on a morally innocent person, society gains when it can hope to facilitate by this method the observance of certain minimum requirements of care.[21]

On the other hand, there is in many systems growing criticism of punishment for "crimes without victims." For what is punished here is behavior deemed morally wrong or abject but which has not disturbed the public order nor trespassed the private sphere of other individuals. (The problems of criminal liability for homosexual acts or fornication offer examples.) In fact many of the crimes without victims involve conflicts between the competing moral views of the dominant culture and deviant subcultures. Hence the courts have the choice between becoming the enforcement agents of the prevailing culture or enforcing laxly.[22]

The traditional legal cultures of the Middle and Far East present a stark contrast to all system which recognize and protect the rights of individuals. They deny that members of the society are entitled to a "struggle for law." [23] In Confucian thought the desirable condition of universal harmony and stability is not to be attained by law or a balance of rights and duties. The central concept of "*li*" envisages a society centered around and ordered solely by duty.[24] The ideal government is not one ruled by good laws but by superior men whose mission consists in teaching people by word and by example how to live virtuously. In a society where *li* prevails, self-interest is placed under an effective control motivated by inner conviction. Hence the virtuous man is himself the source of order. "If men were angels," the Federalist papers stated, there would be no need for a govern-

[21] See Paton, 1972, p. 386, and Friedmann, 1972, pp. 202–207.

[22] Grossman and Sarat, 1971, p. 185.

[23] A classical treatise by the German jurist von Ihering bearing the title *Der Kampf ums Recht* (*The Struggle for Law*) was published in 1873.

[24] *Li* translates as "principle." When used as a verb it means "putting things in order." See also, for what follows, the discussion of traditional legal and political thought in China by Mote, 1968, pp. 394–407, and by Schurman, 1968, pp. 408–24.

ment by law, but the authors took a sceptical view of such an angelic condition. Confucian thought shares with other millenarian visions a belief in the perfectability of men and the abrupt eradication of evil which would permit the elimination of laws as such.[25] If legal rules, *fa*, backed differently from *li* by effective sanctions, had to be relied upon to control disorder, they should never be regarded as more than a temporary expedient.

There have been times in the troubled history of China when such precepts were altogether ignored in favor of a highly developed machinery of rules and compulsion. But since the "legalists" were driven from power in the second century B.C. Confucianism has at all times sufficiently impregnated the slowly developing legal institutions so as to assert at least interstitially the supremacy of *li* and of customs oriented on its commands. When laws on the disposition of property by contract, on inheritance, and on family relations were enacted it was still expected that people would settle such matters outside of court and without insisting on their "rights." The revolution of 1911 and the years of the Kuomintang regime that followed aimed at a massive westernization of the law with the help of foreign advisors. But where codes and laws conflicted with traditional ideas of propriety and equity, they were in fact ignored even when a conflict was submitted to a court.[26]

Until 1957 the Communist regime in China seemed to follow the same path of legal developments that took place in the Soviet Union. This amounted to further westernization of the law: a greater reliance on the courts accompanied by a heightened prestige for the legal profession and by an overall concern for stability through law. But recently this trend has been reversed and then explicitly repudiated. All efforts at codification seemed to have been halted. While at an earlier period concepts such as contracts and torts had been developed, parties are now generally expected to avoid all litigation and to solve whatever conflicts may arise by "arrangement." Instead of enforcing "rights" that may have arisen from tortious liability or from a breach of contract, the authorities will assist people to live in harmony [27]—a goal in accordance with traditional attitudes even if the party mass line condemns Confucianism as reactionary.

In the field of criminal law and procedures the Chinese Communists have operated altogether without a code, again differently from the Soviet and Eastern European regimes. Political crimes and dissent are dealt with harshly and summarily without any concern for the rights of the offender. But other criminal conduct is treated primarily as a social behavior best to be corrected by admonition and reeducation. To awaken a feeling of shame

---

25 See Barkun, 1971, pp. 113ff.

26 David and Brierley, 1968, p. 447.

27 Hazard, 1969, pp. 338–40 and 408–10.

for having violated a social duty is deemed an effective means of rehabilitation. Undoubtedly the internalization of community feelings inherent in the concept of *li* permits the Chinese Communists frequently to dispense with harsher sanctions.[28]

The strong survival of a duty-centered rather than a rights-centered legal culture is particularly impressive in a country as westernized and industrialized as Japan. Behind a facade of Western law, traditional roles and rules have survived. A hierarchical social status, patriarchal rather than despotic, is still defining every individual as being contingent on another; however, this impinges on all legal relationships, including those entered into by contract. It remains largely incompatible with a legal system that is based on fixed and universalistic standards.[29]

The Confucian teaching that the parties' insistence on their rights must be dampened so that one could get them to compromise has left deep marks. As a practical consequence litigation does not appear as a desirable means of conflict solution; in many cases the attempt to have recourse to the courts is considered as a form of extortion. This in turn reflects, in Japan as well as in Communist China, on the status and prestige of the legal profession (see below, Chapters 4 and 5). As in any other highly industrialized society, conflicting interests do of course arise in Japan and are pressing for recognition. But the accepted means of conflict settlement prevents them from being recognized as rights.

Where Hindu law has survived, as in the Indian village community, the traditional legal axiom to conform to the duties incumbent upon one's station in life still prevails. It defeats not only any claim to equality before the law but also results in a summary denial of personal rights.[30]

THE "RULE OF LAW"

"The trouble with you Westerners," a London-educated mainland Chinese lawyer recently uttered, "is that you never got beyond that primitive stage you call the 'rule of law.' . . . China has always known that law is not good enough to govern a society. She knew it twenty-five hundred years ago, and she knows it today."[31]

Indeed since antiquity "Westerners" have discussed as impassionately as inconclusively the relationship between law and power which underlies the concept of the rule of law. Is law merely or mainly a weapon in the hands of those who hold power in state and society? Or is the law forever concerned with intervening in relationships that enable individuals or cor-

---

[28] For a recent analysis of a fluid situation, see Cohen, 1968.

[29] von Mehren, 1963, pp. 43ff.

[30] See Bozeman, 1971, p. 124.

[31] J. Cohen, 1968, p. 4.

porate bodies to compel the will of others? [32] Should a legal system which wishes both to maintain order and to dispense justice disperse power or organize it for the sake of efficiency? Techniques such as federalism and pluralism create multiple power centers in order to meet the dangers of too great a concentration of power. But how far can decentralization be pursued without the law losing its cohesive force? How can the law be enabled to accommodate contradictory demands for scarce goods? Can it ever interfere with previously acquired rights of individuals or groups?

All of these questions show the intimate and truly dialectic relationship between law and power: law is always part principle and part power. If law to fulfill its ends must be backed by power, unchecked power will easily ignore the demands of justice and of security by a capriciousness which makes it impossible to gauge the consequences of one's own or other's behavior. The basic philosophy of constitutionalism as it developed through struggles and controversies in both common-law and civil-law countries at the beginning of modern times implies an understanding of the law as a bond between the citizen and the community. Protected in his rights by the community, the citizen assumes obligations which go beyond his identification with castes, or classes, or groups. The reciprocal relationship thus established assumes concrete form in the law that binds individuals and community in a compact that, symbolically though not historically, resembles a contract. To be sure there is no egality in this partnership between state and individual. But there are recognizable, if not always respected, limits to what the community may do with its power, and there exist procedures which may be invoked when the limits are transgressed. These aspects of Western constitutionalism are referred to in English-speaking countries as the "rule of law" of which *Rechtsstaat* is the German equivalent. Latin countries adhere to the same motion without having coined a special term for it: the concept of *légalité* is both broader and narrower.

If the rule of law is a widely used term in England and the United States, its meaning is often loose and shifting. A common denominator of its various meanings (and of those of *Rechtsstaat* as well) includes an injunction against governmental arbitrariness, a high-level guarantee of "reasonableness" in relations between man and state. Commands should be issued and coercion be applied only on the basis of announced rules. Hence the procedural aspects of the rule of law, described in the constitution of the United States as "due process," are really giving teeth to principle. But due process is not a self-defining or universally valid concept. Through the door of "due process" changing views of natural rights have been introduced in order to criticize or even to invalidate laws which wanted to serve social utility.

[32] Hurst, 1971, pp. 78ff.

In a legal system such as that of the United States which attributes to the courts the power of judicial review, the yardstick of due process has at times defeated legislative purpose in favor of the most conservative groups in society. Similarly German jurists and philosophers prior to the First World War gave to the concept of the *Rechtsstaat* an interpretation which legitimized the practices of an only semiconstitutional monarchy. Yet modern totalitarianism was to demonstrate that by comparison even a shifting concept of the rule of law is still a shield against brutal arbitrariness.

The duty of safeguarding "due process" (or its equivalents in other Western systems) is not solely imposed on the government and its officials. Nongovernmental bodies, such as charities, colleges, trade unions, and corporations, are also formulating and enforcing rules by which men live. (Characteristically and quite correctly their rules are frequently called "by-laws.") They too are required to observe a minimum of procedural safeguards even though the enforcement of such standards will depend on the amount of power and authority which the private organizations have acquired within a given society.

The substance and procedures of the rule of law will always be concerned with relations between authority and the individual. The question of where conflicts between public authorities and individuals should be decided has long divided Anglo-American and civil-law systems. In the former the view has been that the equality of all before the law and thereby the rule of law itself would be violated if suits involving government and administration were not tried in the "common" courts. On the European continent and in Latin America a more or less elaborate hierarchy of administrative tribunals has been developed to decide this kind of controversy. The results of the two approaches have at times been different though the surviving differences are frequently exaggerated. (For a fuller discussion see below, Chapter 6).

The Soviet equivalent to the Western concept of the rule of law is the principle of socialist legality. Over the years the legal order of the Soviet Union and of the Eastern European countries has moved between the poles of flexibility and stability according to the needs of the states and of their economies. But amid frequent changes socialist legality has been announced steadfastly as an indispensable standard to be respected by government officials as well as by people in general.[33] The courts and administrative tribunals, the Control Commissions of the Federal Governments, and also a special hierarchy of officials—the Prokuratura, a czarist institution which was revived in 1922—are presumably the guardians of socialist legality. That the Prokuratura continued to function all through the

---

[33] David and Brierley, 1968, pp. 160ff.

years of Stalin's rule highlights the difference that existed between promise and performance.[34] At present the observation of fair procedures is described as the most important aspect of socialist legality. Soviet attempts to define its substance reveal an almost complete identification of the term with legitimacy: in order to conform to socialist legality the law itself and the institutions that serve it must be accepted as just by popular consensus.

But in all countries, not only in the Soviet Union, the building of such a consensus is a function of the political rather than the legal system.

LEGITIMACY   The exercise of power by legal means must be recognized as legitimate; otherwise it will not be able to fulfill the functions which society has assigned to it. Legitimacy quiets doubts and promotes acceptance not only of specific legal rules, but also of the system that has enacted them. There can be no legitimacy without an organizational structure manned and maintained by "officers of the law" who exercise authority in a prescribed way. While in a developed legal order judges might be considered the most important officers of the law, also a policeman, the chief executive, a legislator, an attorney, a licensing commissioner, or a draft board member are "magistrates" whose actions affect the rights of citizens.[35] Both those who exercise authority and those who are subject to it must share the belief that what is prescribed is desirable or at the very least tolerable; this applied to both substance and procedures.[36] Not only what a government and its legal system can do *for* the people, but also what it can do *to* them, is a question that is answered differently by different political and legal cultures.[37]

If one wants to find out which attitudes seem to connote belief in the legitimacy of a legal order, it is necessary to distinguish between a general acceptance of the law as indispensable and opinions concerning the actual output, especially of legislatures and of courts. A comparative evaluation of such attitudes in different systems and cultures is all but impossible because of a lack of data.

In the dominant culture of the United States it appears that the law has remained until quite recently a "great reservoir of emotionally important symbols" because a widespread need for security "develops the

---

[34] In Solzhenitsyn's grim report on the workings of the Soviet judicial machinery the Prokuratura is not even mentioned!

[35] Selznick, 1968, p. 54.

[36] See Bendix, 1964, p. 20 for an updating of Max Weber's main conclusions.

[37] Verba, 1965, p. 541.

structure of an elaborate dream-world where logic creates justice." [38] To be sure many minority groups in present-day America would deride such feelings and point to their own experiences with the law and its officers. It remains a fact, however, that the best-organized minority groups have used the courts as vehicles for their complaints and eventually as channels for proposed reforms, a means of pressure politics unknown in most other countries. Tocqueville was not the last foreign observer to describe Americans as fairly obsessed with law when he remarked that:

> Scarcely any political question arises in the United States that is not resolved sooner or later into a judicial question. . . . the spirit of the law, which is produced in the schools and courts of justice, gradually penetrates beyond their walls into the bosom of society where it descends to the lowest classes, so that at last the whole people contract the habits and the tastes of the judicial magistrate.[39]

A recent study concluded, on the basis of a wealth of empirical research, that in the United States law was *the* "national ideology." [40]

Certainly, to place such a high value on the law "in general" may be regarded as a legitimizing attitude of some importance. But Americans will also express considerable scepticism about the concrete role which their courts are playing in implementing generally recognized ends of the law. According to a poll conducted in 1969, 79 percent of the general public were convinced that the courts treated the rich better than the poor and 40 percent felt that blacks fared worse than whites (among black respondents the corresponding figures were 86 and 66 percent).[41] While these answers indicate that economic discrimination is regarded as more prevalent than racial prejudice, all figures mirror a low confidence in judicial neutrality. It is true that a 1967 poll concerned with attitudes towards the Supreme Court obtained rather strikingly different results: when asked whether they thought the Supreme Court had been impartial in its decisions or tended to favor one group more than others 47 percent described the Court as impartial, 30 percent as playing favors. A fairly extensive study concluded that in 1966 two out of three people thought that the Supreme Court was doing its job very well. Yet the authors concluded that the support given to the Supreme Court was to be described as "diffuse"

[38] Arnold (1935), 1962, p. 34. The author was one of President Roosevelt's main "trust-busters."

[39] Tocqueville (1835), 1957, vol. I, p. 290.

[40] McCloskey, 1964, p. 361.

[41] Blumenthal et al., 1972, p. 60f.

and that the level of information was low.[42] Yet another poll (1964) indicated that only 12 percent of the respondents had liked what the U.S. Supreme Court had done "in the past few years"; 26 percent expressed dislike and a full 57 percent said that they were not interested in the Court's activities. Morever these figures should be evaluated in light of the fact that the same poll revealed a very low understanding of the Court's activities. Most of those that were favorably inclined towards the Court's output held unrealistic views about the judicial process which in their opinion engaged in value-free and merely mechanical decision-making. The better informed respondents were to be found most of the time among those most critical of the Court.[43]

In England, former confidence in the courts is shaken. A Gallup poll found that whereas in 1961 63 percent of the respondents felt that English courts dispensed justice impartially, two years later the percentage had dropped to 47 percent. An increasing number of people believed that the English courts favored the "rich and influential." [44]

Very similar feelings have been recorded in other countries of Western Europe. According to an unpublished German poll 42 percent of the respondents were of the opinion that "common people" did not get the same treatment by the courts as the wealthy; 50 percent believed that "jurists" were only aggravating difficulties in daily life. A comparable poll in France (1972) revealed that 42 percent of respondents believed judges were favoring the rich, and 49 percent considered them to be "equitable." Among working class respondents the respective opinions were 48 and 44 percent. (Legislation fared worse: 58 percent characterized laws as favoring the rich; only 35 percent adjudged them to be equitable.) In the French Fifth Republic the proportion of those who believed that the judicial system was functioning badly has varied between 60 and 48 percent; never more than 35 percent, and often fewer, thought that it was working well.[45]

These contradictions, similar to those revealed in polls conducted in the United States, must raise doubts about the appropriateness of opinion surveys for reaching a reliable judgment of public attitudes toward the legitimizing role of the courts. Actual behavior might be worth scrutiny if one wishes to evaluate the citizens' contribution to the maintenance of the system. When they seek judicial settlement of conflicts the parties involved demonstrate that in their opinion the functioning and the output

---

[42] Devine, 1972, pp. 164f., and Grossman and Tanenhaus, 1969, pp. 295f.

[43] Dolbeare, 1967, pp. 201ff.

[44] Polling results quoted here are from Abel-Smith and Stevens, 1967, p. 304.

[45] Ehrmann, 1971, p. 318.

of the legal system can claim legitimacy, even though the parties might be critical of concrete court decisions.[46]

In many a nation's history the struggle for recognition of new legal rules has been a significant event. Success or failure is not always merely a function of the respective strength of political forces.. Traits of the legal culture and the legitimacy attributed to its values may often have determined the outcome. However, to isolate the independent and dependent variables in such situations and to compare them systematically is an exacting task which has not really been undertaken.

The greatest shortcomings of available information and analysis stem in part from the fact that almost invariably legal systems are treated as a homogeneous unit, while in fact legal subcultures not only live by different rules but also have a different outlook on the significance and the reach of the law. A recent study of the multiplicity of legal levels and systems states:

> *Any human society . . . does not possess a single consistent legal system, but as many such systems as there are functioning sub-groups. Conversely, every functioning sub-group of a society regulates the relations of its members by its own legal system, which is of necessity different, at least in some respects, from those of other sub-groups.*[47]

If this is true in highly developed countries such as the United States or Japan, then in developing countries the law and courts must as yet do very little to integrate people into a homogeneous legal culture. (For additional details, see Chapter 7.)

There exists in all societies, whatever their stage of development, the danger that the gap between the living and the official law will become too wide. At some point divisive centrifugal forces could bring about the disintegration of the legal culture and its processes. To prevent this all systems have recourse to a variety of conciliatory devices, among them the participation of laymen in the administration of justice and new grievance procedures (to be discussed below in Chapters 5 and 6).

---

[46] See Grossman and Sarat, 1971, pp. 203ff. for an excellent discussion of some of the questions raised in the text.

[47] Pospisil, 1967, p. 3.

THE MEN AND WOMEN OF THE LAW

4

THE LEGAL NOTABLES Incipient legal orders can usually get along without specialists who have acquired through appropriate training a knowledge of substantive legal rules and procedures. But when a society becomes more heterogeneous, norms will become more abstract and more universal so that they can reconcile the interests and values of the various groups making up the community. By the same token the tasks of settling disputes or of advising on their possible settlement becomes more difficult and requires special training.[1] There emerges then in almost all societies a fairly well defined and stratified group, the legal notables.

The professionals of the law cannot help but shape the structure and style of any legal system and determine much of the climate in which it functions. Since there is a close affinity of legal system and societal values, legal notables can generally be expected to share the prevalent value system: their recruitment, training, and socialization will be directed at producing such accordance. Legal elites are everywhere and "almost by definition the embodiment of . . . prevailing values in that they control the sanctions with which the conformist is rewarded and the deviant punished."[2]

Most modern legal systems, once they have become independent of direct control by religious or political agencies, will have need for the following categories of notables [3] and will therefore provide for an adequate

[1] Abel, 1974, p. 288.

[2] Dahrendorf, 1964, pp. 270f.

[3] Similarly, with some differences, Mayhew, 1968, pp. 62f. He follows in all essentials Max Weber's pathbreaking analysis of the legal *honoratiores;* see Weber, (1922) 1954, pp. 198–223.

supply of them even though what is deemed adequate may vary greatly in different cultures. The first group is made up of all those who are adjudicators of legal conflicts; foremost among them are the judges and magistrates, but also arbitrators, examiners, officials sitting on quasi-judicial bodies and on administrative tribunals, etc. The second group, the advocates, appear before the adjudicating agencies of whatever kind as representatives of the parties involved. The latter may be private individuals or groups. In criminal and administrative proceedings the public interest is represented by district attorneys, public prosecutors, and the like. A third group acts as legal advisors, usually without appearing before courts or tribunals; this group includes the British solicitor, the French *avoué*, the Soviet jurisconsultant, or, in many systems, the notary. Legal scholars make up a fourth group in those countries where adjudicating agencies rely on them as expert witnesses. Their more common function of training oncoming generations of legal specialists also gives them important characteristics as legal notables. A fifth group, very heterogeneous but increasingly important, is made up of legally trained personnel employed either in government service or by private business.

Although these categories correspond to the main functions which the legal *honoratiores* have to assume in all modern systems, the division of tasks is not always the same. The division might be more or less sharp—the status and prestige accorded the various groups, as well as their recruitment and training, might differ greatly. In many systems, but to different extents, law jobs are filled by laymen whose legal training is either nil or rudimentary. While they assume important and possibly indispensable tasks, they are not to be counted among the legal "notables" discussed in this chapter. (On their participation in the judicial process, see below, Chapter 5).

For all of these and connected reasons statistical data about the number of trained lawyers in a given country and about their distribution among the various categories—judges, attorneys, prosecutors, etc.—are of little use for comparative purposes. Frequently such data are misleading rather than revealing about contrasting traits of different legal systems. As just one example, litigiousness, the propensity of a population to settle its disputes through the judicial process, is a cultural characteristic of considerable interest (to be discussed in Chapter 5). But one attempt to establish a connection between a society's litigation rate and the number of attorneys available in a given country had to conclude that the relationship was insignificant.[4] Hence where the following descriptive analysis of legal positions in a number of countries mentions some figures to illustrate points, our caveat should be kept in mind.

[4] See Grossman and Sarat, 1973, p. 5.

Undoubtedly there is no other country in the world that has as many legally trained men and women per capita of population as the United States. Their number is presently estimated at more than 325,000, or one out of every 270 gainfully employed persons. Somewhat fewer than 10,000 of these serve as full-time judges at the federal, state, or municipal levels. An additional 40,000 are employed at the various levels of government. Business firms employ more than 30,000 as house lawyers, and law schools employ about 2,500 on their teaching staffs. The rest, and hence a large majority of legally trained personnel, are attorneys-at-law, but not all of them are exclusively in private practice.

The most striking difference between the organization of the legal profession in the United States and in the United Kingdom is the compartmentalization of British attorneys into barristers and solicitors. A somewhat similar division was until recently also known in a civil-law system such as France, while other continental countries, Germany among them, ignore it.

The strict formality of the medieval law suits in England and in France made it indispensable that plaintiff as well as defendant be accompanied in court by a legally trained assistant who would voice his party's pleas and defenses. (The French *a-vocat* and its earlier German equivalent *Fürsprecher* describe this function very well.) The complicated machinery of justice would easily have been stalled if those appearing in court had not been well trained. At least in England the ensuing close relationship between the bench and the bar (the generic names for the judges and the "bar"risters) has endured until this day.[5] It has also marked off the barristers as a special elite of the profession. An even more prestigious and hence particularly coveted rank of senior barristers, the Q.C.s (Queen's Counselors), was created by the Stuarts in the seventeenth century. Until fairly recently "silk," the special garment worn by the Q.C.s, was regarded principally as a reward for political loyalty rather than as evidence of legal competence. But the British talent for turning medieval ornaments into functional modern institutions has now made the Q.C.s into the main reservoir for important judgeships (see below).

On the other hand the fact that most English courts were sitting only in London obligated litigants to turn for help and advice to another group of lawyers, the solicitors, who would prepare the case, gather the evidence, and set the court procedure into motion. This tradition has survived: today a client can approach the inner group of not more than 3,000 highly trained barristers (for the whole country) only through the outer group of general practitioners of whom there are about 30,000 (still a small number when compared with the United States). A very large part of the solicitors'

[5] See also for what follows Abel-Smith and Stevens, 1968, pp. 38–63.

business is concerned with conveyances transferring all sorts of private property. It is mainly for this reason that the solicitors are frequently referred to as the social workers of the middle classes.

What appears extraordinary is the survival rather than the genesis of the strict division between the two groups. While there are some practical reasons that explain its origins, the division also suited a highly stratified society inclined to create wherever possible small and specialized elites. The process reached its culmination in Victorian times:

> *Each branch of the profession evolved its own tight organisation. Each organisation laid down its own strict standards for entry. Both established detailed codes of regulations and practice to govern their dealings with the public and with each other.*[6]

Customs and habits established and solidified in an age of an unbridled business civilization and individualism have not been overturned in a welfare society. A parallel, and certainly connected, particularity of the legal profession in Great Britain is the absence of legally trained personnel in other callings. In most countries, (in democracies as well as in authoritarian regimes), law school graduates are to be found in a great variety of jobs and are therefore playing a prominent and occasionally dominant position in society (see below). Such a mobility, which frequently permits a cross-fertilization of experience, is largely unknown in Great Britain. While this is often criticized, the division of the profession is not; quite typically even those bent on reforms still think that the fusion of the two branches of the profession would produce more public ill than good.[7]

If the top strata of the legal profession in Great Britain continue to enjoy a higher status and prestige than their brethren in other countries, this seems due to their homogeneity in origin, training, and outlook rather than to their function in society. Such homogeneity, however, is admirably served by a highly selective and hence numerically restricted corps of specialists who monopolize communications with that part of the judiciary that matters. Whether this kind of personnel malthusianism serves the best interests of the "consumers," that is, those who are in need of legal services, is of course doubtful. It is frequently pointed out that barristers as well as solicitors are losing touch with the mainstream of litigation. This is the foremost reason why administrative tribunals and other quasi-legal courts have come to occupy an even more important part in the legal life of Great Britain than in other countries. (For more details see below, Chapter 8.)

[6] Finer (himself a Q.C.), 1970, p. 45.

[7] Ibid., p. 49, but also Jackson, 1967, p. 362.

In France the *avoués* have long played a role similar to that of the solicitors. But recently the *avoués* and the attorneys, the *avocats,* have been merged into a single group. There are now about 10,000 *avocats,* of whom almost half practice in Paris, a striking indication of the country's centralization. But the *notaires* pictured realistically in numerous nineteenth-century novels continue to be indispensable to the bourgeoisie of which they are part and parcel.

The notaries of France and some other civil-law countries like Italy and Spain have nothing but the name in common with the notary public of the United States. While he is not concerned with litigation the notary's services are needed for a great many transactions bound to specific forms. Notaries are, as a French panegyrist described them, "at the origin and end of all things in civil life, as the priest is in the religious order."[8] In rural France and in smaller towns the notary acts as a general advisor to his clients—for their marriage contracts as well as for their last wills—in much the same manner as a family solicitor in England. Since their number is also restricted (about 6,300 for the whole of France), they often have large offices with numerous clerks. A notary's office is frequently a lucrative business sold upon the notary's death or retirement at prices fixed by the Ministry of Justice. The Province of Quebec furnishes a good illustration of how intimately the organization of the legal profession and the availability of notables are connected with the technicalities of the legal system. As in other parts of Canada, the recruitment of the provincial judges follows essentially the English pattern (see below), but the *notaires* play the same role and have the same prestige as in France, because the contractual and other legal relations between individuals must rely on their services.

In contrast to their English and formerly their French colleagues, the American attorney-at-law and the German *Rechtsanwalt* combine the preparation of a case and its presentation in the courtroom. They also function as general legal advisor of their clients, and this activity might in fact occupy most of their time. In the United States as well as in Europe the number of individual practitioners is dwindling although only the United States has developed the mammoth law offices which divide the work functionally among specialists to the point of ignoring a client's wish for the services of a particular lawyer. In some civil-law countries, especially in South America, no partnerships among attorneys are tolerated since they are considered a violation of the individualized and confidential relationship between a client and his lawyer. An in-between solution has been sought among solicitors in Great Britain and generally in Western Europe where a limited number of attorneys pool office resources but continue

---

[8] Quoted here from Zeidlin, 1973, p. 43. An entire chapter of his book (pp. 43–52) is devoted to the role of the notaries in nineteenth-century and present-day France.

to serve individual parties. Yet complaints about the inadequacy of such arrangements and especially about insufficient specialization are frequent.

Large business concerns overcome these shortcomings by employing a legal staff of their own just as governments do. The modern corporation lawyer has become an ubiquitous phenomenon. Whatever his legal skills, and they are usually considerable, he will not only be expected to share the values of his clients, but he also fulfills the function of a high-class messenger between other elites in society. What has been observed particularly in the United States is probably true of most technologically advanced countries: top-flight attorneys can be drawn upon as "a vast reservoir of actual or potential information about the social and political topography. . . ." [9]

A recent development in the United States has been termed the "explosion of advocacy"; however, a parallel phenomenon has arisen in other postindustrialist societies. What is involved here is more than a substantial increase of legal services of the most varied kind to those in need of advice and assistance. In many countries legal aid to the indigent has been established or enlarged by legislation or voluntary activities. But more than that, the older emphasis on serving individual clients and on developing the law through the advocacy of single cases is being supplemented and sometimes supplanted by providing services to an organization which in turn represents the interests of an entire group. Such groups may comprise a neighborhood, a racial minority, a professional calling, or activists fighting for a cause. "As individual demands become organized *strategic advocacy* develops: the lawyer can select and possibly generate issues for the purpose of challenging practices and pressing recognition of new rights." [10] All those involved in this process—the parties, attorneys, and judges—will easily address themselves to broad questions of policy and to an ascertainment of the interests involved. This in turn furthers a legal development which is no longer dependent on single disputes but which can evolve in a more systematic and planned fashion.

At one time in the United States it appeared that the challenge of becoming this kind of an "action lawyer" would deprive the large prestigious law firms of top talent. In a number of countries the simultaneous growth of novel professional organization, to be discussed below, could lend permanence to the new orientation of the practicing lawyer. But it appears that the reformatory zeal of the new advocates is frequently broken by the weight of an essentially conservative profession which is still strong enough to dampen unorthodox efforts when they continue for too long.

[9] Quoted here from Riesman, 1954, p. 451.

[10] Nonet and Carlin, 1968, p. 72. The entire article and the literature quoted in it are relevant for this phenomenon.

In the Soviet Union attorneys were viewed with some distrust even after the original design of doing without law and without lawyers had been abandoned with the introduction of the New Economic Policy (NEP). The lingering diffidence was probably due to the somewhat "bourgeois" flavor inherent in the private relationship between client and attorney. Yet little by little the attorneys' prestige, and corresponding income, have grown, even though by Western standards their activities in both civil and criminal matters remain limited. Many Soviet attorneys work in collectives which try deliberately to depersonalize the relationship between client and attorney. The collective's director assigns cases to members of his staff independently of a client's wishes. In certain respects these collectives resemble the large law offices of the United States.

The fact that about 60 percent of the 12,000 to 15,000 practicing attorneys in the Soviet Union are reported to be party members gives an indication of a somewhat less than outstanding elite status. Probably party membership is higher among the about 60,000 jurists who are employed at various levels of the administration (including state enterprises). By contrast, all of the professionally trained Soviet judges in 1963 (between 8,000 and 9,000) were either party members or candidates for party membership.

A rather original group of Soviet lawyers are the 30,000 "jurisconsults." In as much as they give legal advice rather than appear before courts they could be likened to solicitors or *avoués*. However, most of their advice is requested by state enterprises, by labor unions, and by similar organizations. In recent years the number of jurisconsults has grown rapidly; moreover, leading members of this group are reported to have played a dominant role in the preparation of new legislation concerning the activities of Soviet firms.[11] There is some resemblance between the activities of the jurisconsults and the action lawyers in the United States.

Because of its breadth the institution that is often called the cornerstone of the Soviet legal profession has no equivalent in the legal systems of the West. When the office of the Prokuratura was created by Peter the Great it was described as "the eyes of the monarch"; in 1922 it was again found opportune to organize such an office.[12] In civil and especially in criminal matters its members assume the functions which elsewhere are performed by public prosecutors, district attorneys, and the attorney general. But at the same time, as the presumed guardian of socialist legality (see above, Chapter 3), the Prokuratura exercises a general supervision

[11] For more details see Barry and Berman in Skilling and Griffiths, eds., 1971, pp. 306f.

[12] See the lengthy discussion in David and Brierley, 1968, pp. 161ff. and in Skilling and Griffiths, eds., 1971, pp. 311ff.

and can rescind unlawful decisions by state officials including judicial decisions. The Prokatura may even institute a recourse against a decision by the U.S.S.R. Supreme Court by appealing it to the Praesidium. It is quite in line with such plenitude of powers that the Prokuratura, unlike the prosecuting authorities in most other systems, is not subject to the hierarchical control of the Union-Republican Ministry of Justice. For all these reasons the office attracts the most able legal personnel; its staff now numbers about 17,000 to 18,000, which is about twice the number of full-time judges.

In the past another group of notables, the legal scholars, frequently had a decisive influence on long-range developments of the law and on the outcome of concrete disputes as well. The Roman jurisconsults, usually gentlemen of leisure, laid the groundwork for a tradition which was revived in the Renaissance and had its equivalent in countries of Moslem civilization. In early modern Europe the teachers of law were not only men of profound learning but also men with creative minds. Their role was probably greatest in Germany, Italy, and Latin America, while the early development of a judicial caste in France destroyed the close collaboration between judges and scholars. Germans boasted of possessing a *Professorenrecht* which they judged to be superior to the French *Juristenrecht*. Even today the parties to a suit in a civil-law country may demand or submit an expert brief by a professorial specialist on a point of law. At least in Germany scholarly treatises are respected and quoted by attorneys as well as in judicial decisions. In turn the law professors stay closer to the practice of law and are thereby less dogmatic; this enhances their ability to have a say in the development of the law.[13] In this respect, the Soviet Union follows continental traditions: the prestige and the weight of law professors are far higher than that of other jurists; this is particularly remarkable in view of their small number.

In Great Britain, with the significant exception of Scotland, legal scholarship has in spite of its excellence never played a similarly important role. This is mostly due to the particularities of legal education and the ensuing close relationship between bar and bench (to be discussed below). An outstanding scholar such as John Austin resigned his professorship at the University of London at age 43 utterly discouraged by dwindling audiences. William Blackstone's monumental textbook, the *Commentaries on the Laws of England,* became an authority in revolutionary and post-revolutionary America rather than in England; in England judges preferred to rely on the dicta and rulings of their brethren and predecessors, the notables they recognized and respected. Only lately are learned treatises

---

[13] In Latin America law professors who are also practicing lawyers are known for a curious kind of schizophrenia: they will be aggressively doctrinaire as professors but naturally pragmatic in their other role (see Merryman, 1969, pp. 116f.).

which try to extract some principles from the mass of forms and precedents commanding more attention.

The greater prestige which legal scholarship acquired almost at once in the new United States resulted from the difficulties that a far larger and less homogeneous country had to face when it sought to give to its legal system a coherence which in England had accrued naturally. The early establishment and growing importance of law schools gave weight to the opinions of the teachers of law who often were also active practitioners. The foremost law reviews and textbooks facilitated scholarly communication across state borders and furthered a common outlook at least on federal and on the surviving common law. The recruitment of upper-level judges from the ranks of legal scholars is not infrequent in the United States and, for that matter, in Germany, while it is practically unknown in England.

TRAINING AND SOCIALIZATION

The young French lawyer and aristocrat sent across the ocean by his government to study the prison system of the New World reflected on the legal profession he encountered during his travels:

> *The special information which lawyers derive from their studies ensures them a separate station in society; and they constitute a sort of privileged body in the scale of intelligence. . . . they naturally constitute a body; not by any previous understanding, or by an agreement which directs them to a common end; but the analogy of their studies and the uniformity of their methods connect their minds as a common interest might combine their endeavours.* [14]

On the pages that follow these remarks Tocqueville elaborated on his insight into the relationship between legal training and legal mentality in various cultural and political settings. It is quite true that different methods of learning, what there is to learn about the law and about its operation, and the training which the future legal notables are undergoing all reflect the particularities of a legal system and have their impact on its development as well.

As classical Rome had done before, England has for centuries given to its top group of legal specialists, the barristers, from among whom the country's judges also are chosen, a practical and essentially nonacademic training. The four Inns of Court, all in London, have been described as the last survival in Europe of a medieval republican oligarchy. They are law school, professional organization, and a tightly knit social club, all in one.

[14] Tocqueville (1835) 1957, p. 283 (emphasis in the original).

The professional training received at the Inns is added onto a common education which almost all of the aspiring barristers have previously shared in the best public (i.e., private) schools and colleges of the country. The relationship between the masters and the apprentices of the craft, between the experienced and the fledgling practitioners, resembles even today in many respects the relationships in a medieval guild. The Masters and Readers of the Inns of Court are neither university professors nor jurists writing commentaries, but practicing judges and lawyers whose teaching is tied directly to the work of the courts. Training by apprenticeship and learning a field as a craft rather than as a science are by nature conservative methods. They are also apt to promote an unquestioning esprit de corps, shunning controversies which academic study will never entirely avoid. Law taught in this way has been called "tough law," and it was in part this toughness which enabled English law to resist successfully a reception of the Roman law when it swept over Europe during the Renaissance.

Oxford and Cambridge saw little reason to include a training such as it was practiced at the Inns into their teaching programs. Only extraneous subjects, legal history, jurisprudence, and Roman and ecclesiastical law were considered part of a liberal education to be provided by the universities. Later attempts which the universities made to carve themselves a place in legal education were stubbornly resisted by the Masters at the Inns. Like masters of other guilds they obviously feared that a more systematic and rational training might wrest from them "secrets of the trade" which were economically profitable to them. In fact some of the medieval-like and costly procedures of modern English law have been preserved through traditions maintained by the Inns.

The enduring division of the legal profession was partly created and then constantly reproduced by this form of legal education. Only future barristers were given the opportunity of a "pupillage" at the Inns; for the far more numerous group of solicitors a less elitist, and at times fairly shoddy, preparation was for a long time considered adequate. If eventually the University of London and later provincial universities started offering courses in practical legal subjects, these were mostly designed for training solicitors. Yet as late as the thirties "academic lawyers in the universities had, at least compared with the Continent and North America, no real influence in the profession and, again with a few exceptions, were looked down on by members of the other [academic] disciplines." [15]

Since the Second World War the extension of legal services and the corresponding (still modest) increase in the number of legal practitioners have opened new opportunities for aspirants to prepare for the various examinations qualifying them for practice as barristers or solicitors. The

[15] Abel-Smith and Stevens, 1968, p. 58.

instruction at the Inns of Court has been modernized and given a somewhat less corporatist aspect. But according to a critical observer:

> *The history of legal education continued after the Second World War to be mainly a history of vocational training. The law, as a field of academic study, continued to be tolerated rather than encouraged by the legal profession. Training for legal practice was provided in chambers and offices as it had been since the Middle Ages.*[16]

Some changes are now in the offing and the entire field of legal education is in ferment. More undergraduates are reading law. The Colleges of Further Education, institutions of adult education, are now engaging in formal legal instruction. But the place of academic learning, the role of the "cramming schools" (some of them quite famous), and the future of the pupillage are still uncertain. The continuing sharp division between two groups of practicing lawyers, discussed above, is obviously reflected in such uncertainties. Altogether the traditional outlook still has an impact on the operations of the law and on the preparation of lawyers.

When Tocqueville described his impressions of the American lawyers he had encountered, he called them, quite admiringly, an "aristocracy" and a "counterpoise to democracy." Sometime earlier Jefferson, in a different frame of mind, had referred to them as that "subtle corps of sappers and miners constantly working underground to undermine the foundations of our confederated republic." [17]

Yet by comparison with Old England the temper of nineteenth-century New England, not to mention the expanding continent to the West, was egalitarian and the political system decentralized enough not to emulate the English method of training. Gradually the formalized apprenticeship inherited from colonial times was replaced by law schools, which were established by attorneys who had proven gifted educators and who derived additional income from opening their courses to students from every state in the nation.[18] When a genuinely American legal culture emerged with the advent of Jacksonian democracy guildlike procedures of training were considered altogether inappropriate. In order to forestall a disastrous lowering of standards, established colleges and universities rather than private law schools were given an increasingly important role in legal education. The outcome was a system which stands midway between the English approach

---

[16] Abel-Smith and Stevens, 1967, p. 349.

[17] Quoted here from Dahl, 1967, p. 150.

[18] Stevens, 1971, p. 413. This is (pp. 405–548) the best monograph on the history of the law schools in the United States. For the general relationship between the teachers and the practitioners of the law, see also Auerbach, 1971, pp. 551–601.

to legal training and the academic preparation which lawyers must undergo in civil-law countries.

At all times the autonomy of the American law school within the university organization has been far greater than that of the law faculties in European or Latin American universities. Autonomy, however, has meant frequently not only physical separation but also a lack of intellectual cross-fertilization, if not a complete absence of contact. Moreover, two institutional arrangements, pioneered by Harvard and rapidly adopted throughout the country, were most instrumental in turning the preparation of lawyers into a field of professional training rather than of academic study: (1) the requirement that a liberal education must precede the study of law "liberated," as it were, the law school from paying attention to a study of the basic and general problem underlying law and politics; and (2) the case method, which was considered the most appropriate means of teaching and learning, shaped the minds and outlook of teachers and students alike.

To acquire a knowledge of legal principles by the study of leading cases concentrates attention on practical arrangements and their consequences. Litigation and the outcome of controversies, rather than the implementation of societal values, appear as the center of legal life. The structure of the common law, built on precedent and suspicious of long-range legislative purposes, undoubtedly favors the case-law approach which frequently provides a learning experience not very different from that gained in the Inns of Law.

Criticism of the American law-school curriculum has been endemic and historically has come from many sides. Complaints were often heard that the high intellectual skills of the graduates of the best law schools were frequently not matched by the cultural breadth which one expects from an elite. Recently the common denominator of most reform proposals and actual curriculum changes has been a deemphasis though not the abandonment of the case method, a desire to give greater emphasis to the study of legal policies rather than merely of techniques, to jurisprudential concepts and issues rather than to the fashioning of a professional tool. On the other hand there was concern that to change methods and curriculum might run counter to the students' need to be adequately prepared for the bar examination. As in England, but differently from civil-law countries, these examinations are controlled entirely by the organized profession, not by academic teachers. The constant scrutiny by the American Bar Association of law-school standards appears indispensable, but it skews the training of the American lawyer toward professional preparation rather than toward the mastery of an intellectual discipline.

It is easily understood why legal training at the London Inns of Court has been so effective in providing a strong and largely uniform socialization for the top group of the profession. It transmits cultural values together with the knowledge of legal technicalities to a socially homogeneous group. In the United States the socialization of future lawyers is as uneven as is the instruction at the hundreds of American law schools. It is true that the foremost law schools in the country surpass all modern educational institutions anywhere in aspiring at multifaceted excellence and in producing competitive pressures among students. Instruction and extra-instructional activities, not always free of tediousness, result in molding the fresh and keen minds which the highly selective schools have admitted. Yet at least in recent times complete uniformity is neither expected nor achieved. For the most talented graduates their clerkship with appellate judges, frequently at the highest echelon, continues the process of education. Given the different temperaments and career patterns of these judges, the master-apprenticeship which prevails is of the highest order; it reproduces and maintains a fairly large degree of diversity among the American legal profession. Nonetheless certain "conservativizing" aspects of their training have an impact on most American law-school graduates.[19] One is the tendency, acquired early in law school, to assimilate everything that happens to what has gone before. Another is the "case mentality," a primary focus on what the law *is* and on the costs of compliance or noncompliance with judicial rulings.

As an "ideal type" (which is not necessarily congruent with reality) the university education at a European or Latin American law faculty meets the requirements of Max Weber's category of a rationally trained specialist. Many continental law schools were founded and developed by princes and other local rulers for utilitarian rather than academic reasons: they were to prepare the lawyers and administrators for their service at court. However, the professional interests of the professors who were mostly scholars in a field traditionally tied to philosophy and theology, the intellectual needs of their students arriving in the law faculties directly from their secondary schooling, and the close integration of these faculties in established universities combined to make the instruction far more academic than in the common-law countries. Moreover certain characteristics of the civil law, a deductive bent paying more attention to general categories than to single precedents, seemed to make it imperative to develop the student's "legal grasp" and his power of analysis rather than his knowledge of techniques.[20] In all cultures the ordering of legal materials for instruction is not only an outcome of the system's particularities but also one of the factors which determine its continuity.

---

[19] Becker, 1964, pp. 102–3.

[20] Ehrenzweig, 1959, p. 5.

In several respects the shortcomings of legal training in civil-law countries are the opposite of those complained of in England and in the United States. Frequently lectures given before large audiences may amount to exercises in formal logic or deal with institutional history. They fail to convey the realities of legal life or to discuss the social and political problems behind such realities. What is presented as value-free and "pure" legal science is more often than not an ideological defense of the *status quo*.[21] Though the instruction in American law schools appears unsystematic to the European law professor, it is still more akin to the insights of the various social sciences than many lecture courses in European and Latin American faculties. Entire fields, such as industrial relations, might not be given an adequate place in the curriculum as long as they are regulated by collective bargaining rather than by legislation. There are as yet hardly any equivalents to learning situations common in American law schools, such as a student-edited law review, moot court, or legal aid clinics manned by students. It is true that the educational reforms asked for in both common- and civil-law countries would, if carried out, result in a considerable narrowing of the existing gap.

The number of students attending European and Latin American law schools without any definite intent of entering the legal profession is high. They choose law as a field of study because as it is being taught it is sufficiently broad not to require specific skills or interests but to provide a general training and a diploma which give access to many elite positions in their society. A qualified German observer has described his country's present-day law faculties as the "functional equivalent of British public schools," that is, as providing a gentlemanlike education which cannot be acquired in the (by now) more democratic secondary schools. And he added:

> While in Britain there is considerable emphasis on the technical and pro-
> fessional side of legal training, Germany tends to the other extreme. The
> future members of the German upper class learn [in law school] the values
> of their society at the same time as the allure and technique of elite
> status.[22]

What many members of the German elites in business, public service, politics, and some other callings have in common is their education at the country's law schools, all affiliated with the most prestigious state universities. Similar career patterns are followed in other countries. Until the Second World War the faculties of Japanese universities were in fact training academies for civil servants. Very few of the graduates chose to become judges or attorneys.

---

[21] Merryman, 1969, pp. 65–72.

[22] Dahrendorf, 1964, pp. 301 and 306.

In France the young men and women who aspire to top positions in the civil service through specialized training at the École Nationale d'Administration (ENA) will frequently acquire a law degree "on their way up" without ever considering either bench or bar as a career; theirs might indeed be a certain contempt for the law and its professionals. Until recently most of the training in economics was dispensed in France by the Faculties of Law.

Most Europeans who choose a legal career, however, cannot enter the profession as either judges or attorneys with merely a theoretical law-school education. Years of internship and apprenticeship in a wide variety of juridical assignments will follow. While the length of the training periods, the amount of specialization, and the methods of acquiring practical knowledge vary in different countries, these years provide everywhere an additional experience of effective socialization into what remains, with some remarkable exceptions, a uniformly conservative profession. Since the war France has formalized the instruction of those who wish to compete for the positions of judgeships or public prosecutors (the latter called the *Parquet*): the École Nationale de la Magistrature, at Bordeaux, fashioned after the ENA, was established to improve the preparation for and thereby the prestige of the judiciary. In spite of an interesting curriculum, the school for judges has never acquired the status of the school for bureaucrats and has periodically been shaken by crises. Especially since the events of May-June 1968, the young men and women at the school have questioned not only some of the assumptions underlying their training and its style, but also the traditional role of the French judiciary. If the students at the ENA have so far been little upset by doubts, this is probably to be explained by the fact that the prestige and effectiveness of the high bureaucracy are intact while those of the judiciary are badly shaken. The discontent of the future judges, at times expressed openly, is not to the government's liking; some of the difficulties which the school has encountered in recruiting suitable candidates are described as induced by the government which seems to prefer a scarcity of judges to the influx of reform-minded talent.[23] Several times during recent years the number of women graduates from the school has almost equalled that of men, although the "femininization" of the judiciary which is sometimes heralded with either glee or scorn is still a long way off.

Japan has imitated the French example of a special training institute for judges apparently with great success. Excellent instruction is credited for a noticeable increase in prestige for a profession which by law-school graduates was rated far below a career in the administration.

In some countries which do not adhere strictly to either the common-law or the civil-law traditions, theoretical instruction and practical experience are combined. In Sweden and the Soviet Union, for instance, all mem-

[23] Casamayor, 1973c.

bers of the legal profession must undergo periodically a form of continuing education in fields and duties other than those of their regular positions. According to reports this establishes close contacts between the various categories of practitioners and at the same time prevents the profession from becoming a self-sufficient caste.

When the Cultural Revolution swept China all law schools were closed just as they were at the beginning of the French Revolution. But in China they were not reopened when the universities resumed teaching.

SOCIALIZATION AND RECRUITMENT

Of all the law jobs to be filled in a society judgeships are the most critical. The methods of recruitment for judges will be intimately connected with the legal and political culture. Inasmuch as they determine the kind of personnel who will serve as adjudicators of a great variety of public and private disputes, these methods will shape the development of both the legal and the political system. As has been noted, "recruitment is perhaps the key link between a culture and its judiciary encompassing as it does the means to reinforce old values and inculcate new ones through the socialization of prospective decision-makers." [24]

Among the variables entering the recruitment process in different systems, the following have been identified as the most likely to reflect cultural norms: Who are the key legal or political notables who make the effective choice (rather than the formal appointment)? How much or how little popular participation enters into appointment and control of judges? How important is the role of the judiciary and the organized bar in the selection? How long is the term of judicial office, and how may it be ended? How much professionalization and/or specialization is expected from the persons selected as full-time judges? And who are those most likely to be selected?[25]

No modern legal system could fulfill its legitimizing function or provide for the needed stability and security of expectations if the judicial process were not immunized in some way from directives issued by the executive or other powerholders in society. This requirement is usually formulated as the principle of judicial independence; no regime, except the most forthright totalitarianism, is able to abjure it completely without grave risks. On the other hand, all regimes, whatever their political coloring, expect that the judiciary, for all of its independence, will not stray too far from accepted concepts of the public order. This is true not only when a special kind of justice is dispensed in outright political trials (see below, Chapter 7), but also wherever there is room for judicial discretion, that is, in a fairly large number of civil and criminal suits. To guarantee judicial independence and

[24] Grossman and Sarat, 1971, p. 192.

[25] Ibid., p. 193. The entire article offers an excellent discussion of the relationship of socialization, recruitment, and legal culture.

yet to tame it is the foremost function of the process of selecting judicial officers. In any given system the chosen form of appointment might be tied to the legal culture and political circumstances of a more or less distant past. When changes in the process are introduced, they are usually caused by dissatisfaction with the existing method for selection. Corrections will be made either to strengthen the independence of the judiciary or to prevent too great an autonomy residing in a caste which is out of tune with the convictions of the society it is expected to serve. Sometimes the mere threat of altering procedures may induce incumbent judges to change their way of thinking or at least their style.

The numerous variables listed above as indicators of the connection between legal cultures and the judicial selection process make it obvious that there are many ways of tilting the balance between independence and control. By combining or individualizing various methods a system might attempt to obtain a desired result, although usually the impact might, at least in the short run, be somewhat less effective than expected. There are, however, three basic models of judicial appointments:

1. By choice of the political executive, such as in Great Britain and in the United States for all federal judgeships and for a minority of state judgeships;
2. By direct popular or by indirect elections, a method practiced in the majority of American states, in the Soviet Union, and for many judgeships in Switzerland;
3. Through a civil-servant-like career, the basis of all judicial appointments in continental Europe and other civil-law countries

If these are distinguishable outward forms of appointment they do not by themselves betray the reality of the recruitment process. What matters is upon whose advice an executive appointment is made. Who selects the candidate whose name appears on an election ballot? What security of tenure can a judge expect either by law or by custom? What are the factors deciding promotion in a life-time judicial career?

The appointive method of recruiting judges apparently gives the political executive such exorbitant powers that one might fear for the independence of judges who are selected in this way. But what in fact happens depends on traditions, inalterable or changing, or the political and social setting, and possibly also on the number of positions involved. The British Lord Chancellor (the approximate equivalent of the U.S. Attorney General or a Minister of Justice in other countries) who is responsible for all judicial appointments is himself an active politician. But for at least the last half century earlier habits have been abandoned and he has appointed judges without any regard for their political opinions. Once appointed a judge is expected to steer free of all partisan controversies; the nonpolitical standing of the judiciary has been generally accepted. (In

Quebec, this "sterilization" goes so far as to deprive the judges of their right to vote.) While the Lord Chancellor is entirely free in his selection, he may seek and receive the advice of eminent jurists and judges. But his personal knowledge of a small number of potential candidates will often be sufficient for his choice. In spite of protests members of the bench are still drawn almost exclusively from the ranks of the barristers and most frequently from the senior members, the Q.C.s, which reduces the number of those available for nomination to about 170. Solicitors who come from a far wider social, educational, and political background than their more eminent colleagues are still excluded from major and life-time judicial appointments.

This results in a highly qualified and highly homogeneous—for a modern diversified nation one might say far too homogeneous—group occupying all important judicial positions. In 1963, of 100 high judges, 18 percent were peers or barons; 17 percent came from other nobility; 39 percent came from upper-class families with a strong public-school background; 24 percent came from good middle-class professional families; and only 2 percent came from a humbler background. Eighty-one percent had attended either Oxford or Cambridge, and almost as many had been pupils at one of the foremost public schools.[26]

In the British Commonwealth countries the social background of the judges is far more diversified, but the methods of their appointment are similar. This applies even to a civil-law system like that of Quebec where there is no divided profession as in England. But there too important judgeships are no longer considered political awards and are mostly manned by senior members of the bar, the *bâtonniers*, with the admixture of some law professors.

By comparison the appointment to the (approximately 400) federal judgeships by the American President appears very political. What the English and the American selection processes have in common, and what distinguishes both from countries which rely on a judicial career service, is the fact that lawyers selected for important judgeships usually have a successful professional career behind them. It is indeed such a career that has made them visible and eligible; hence they carry into their new offices a higher initial prestige than what accrues to corresponding positions in Europe.

George Washington was only the first in a long line of presidents who packed the Supreme Court with men they could expect to represent the interests and the point of view of the political coalition which had voted the president into office. One of the most steadfast campaign pledges of Richard Nixon was that he would elevate to the highest bench "strict con-

---

[26] On selection and background of the British judiciary see Abel-Smith and Steven, 1967, pp. 455–58, and Abel-Smith and Steven, 1968, pp. 166–78.

structionists," that is, men who would share his social and constitutional views.

The need for Senate approval of presidential nominations, combined with the practice of what is kindly called "senatorial courtesy," further heightens the political sensitivity of the selection process. In a large and heterogeneous country it also introduces some local and regional norms which strengthen the satisfaction with and thereby the legitimacy of the process. Some of the nomination fights, in which the press and various interest groups participate, have become classics of American political drama, even before Nixon proposed candidates for the Supreme Court who were considered unfit. The nomination of Brandeis in 1916 resulted in "six months of hot blood, cold fury and calculated pressure." [27] The discussions in Congress, the State Houses, and the newspapers about forthcoming judicial appointments make many European observers shudder, committed as they are to a concept of judicial anonymity and neutrality.

The characteristics of the appointment process undoubtedly have their equivalent in differences in the style and nature of the judicial process (to be discussed below in Chapter 6). Yet more than one controversial candidate has emerged from a bitter nomination fight with a considerable amount of independence which he transferred to his new role as a judge. Since a federal judge will generally not expect a promotion, the political sponsorship that brought him to his post loses its impact and he "may be more inclined to consider himself the representative of society at large rather than of its momentary political structure." [28] That Richard Nixon misunderstood this process and thought he could count on "his" nominees for support of his position, was part of his undoing.

Formal requirements for judicial appointment at the federal level are rather minimal and count for even less in appointments to state courts. Nonetheless the American Bar or the State Bar Associations have been given an increasingly important voice in the evaluation of a nominee's qualifications. For federal appointments a respected Association Committee engages in a careful and demanding scrutiny whose results can be ignored only at substantial political peril. The members of big-city law firms which make up the committee therefore fulfill some of the functions assumed by the advisers of the British Lord Chancellor.

The recruitment of judges by election is usually an expression of distrust of a professional caste suspected of serving either their own interests or obeying the injunctions of the political executive. The mockeries of a Rabelais, a Racine, and a Molière give a good indication of the low esteem into which the judiciary of the Ancien Régime had fallen. The French Revolution therefore proceeded to make all judgeships elective and to prescribe to

[27] Hurst, 1950, p. 371.

[28] Kirchheimer, 1961, p. 184.

boot that all deliberations preceding a judcial decision be held in public. The system was soon abolished when concern for "law and order" prevailed.

In the United States Jefferson's and others' distrust of the judiciary had included Federal judges among those officials who could be impeached under article II. 4 of the Constitution. When Tocqueville noted this provision and also that an increasing number of state constitutions, under the impact of Jacksonian populism, made judgeships elective, he was glum: "I venture to predict that these innovations will sooner or later be attended with fatal consequences." [29] Today the institution of elective judgeships has been preserved in two-thirds of the American states (as well as the theoretical possibility of judicial recall in a number of them) as a manifestation of a democratic counterculture designed to balance the traditional Anglo-Saxon practice of appointment by the sovereign at the federal level.[30]

In fact differences between states are so great that it is difficult to generalize. A long-time observer of the judicial system has concluded that if one looks at results rather than at formalities the appointive and the elective methods are no longer very different, especially because of the role professional associations play in both.[31] Such an evaluation is contested at least for those states, and New York is among them, where the nominations are controlled tightly by the party machines. They are not only eliminating primaries but frequently agree on a bipartisan (or nonpartisan) ticket. This leaves the voter no choice whatsoever, but makes the party leadership in fact the appointment agency. Especially in big cities the agreed-upon candidacies are frequently the outcome of ethnic or other group brokerage. Whereas the nominees for federal judgeships are usually first-class lawyers, the professional and moral qualifications of state-court judges are not always high even though Bar Associations also will make recommendations as to the suitability of a candidate on the state level.

A variety of reform models, best known among them the Missouri and the California Plans, have tried to combine the appointive and the elective method: judges are selected by the governor upon the advice of qualified professionals and must face elections after a trial period of one year. Although the American Bar Association has called such a method the "most acceptable substitute available for direct election of judges," it has not been very widely adopted by other states. Everywhere the opposition has come from those political forces which have recognized the compromise as a threat to the patronage aspects of judicial recruitment by election.[32] In numerous states the elective method is enshrined in the constitution and hence not easily altered. Whether new traits in the political culture of the United

[29] Tocqueville (1835), 1957, p. 289.

[30] Grossman and Sarat, 1971, p. 194.

[31] Hurst, 1950, p. 138.

[32] Abraham, 1968, pp. 26–41.

States, among them an impatience with certain party machines, will bring about further changes in the selection methods, remains to be seen.

American occupation authorities undertook an almost touching attempt at effecting cultural impact by import when they insisted that the Japanese constitution accommodate a modified version of the Missouri Plan. All Japanese judges have a civil-servant status like that of judges in other civil-law countries. They are appointed to their position by the government, but the government is advised by the Supreme Court, which actually leaves no choice to the executive and amounts therefore to a straightforward cooptation by the top judicial hierarchy. What is now prescribed is a "people's review," a chance for the voters to recall Supreme Court judges with whom they are dissatisfied. Participation in this ballotting is as high as in general elections but has not yet led to an actual recall.[33]

Among the Western European democracies Switzerland is the only country that seemingly resorts, on the cantonal and the federal level, to either direct or indirect elections. (Some similarities between the style of judicial decision-making in the United States and Switzerland will be discussed below in Chapter 6). So far more than 88 percent of the votes have been in favor of continuing judges in office. Neither the judiciary nor the executive takes a hand in choosing the twenty-six members of the highest federal court. Instead the two houses of the federal parliament function as an electoral college, and the political parties see to it that an agreed quota of the various language communities and of the main parties are represented on the court. Voting is near-unanimous. What appears to be a highly politicized way of selection results nonetheless in a professional magistrature. Whatever have been their political affiliations, all persons chosen have had ample legal, sometimes administrative, and frequently judicial experience. During recent decades professional qualifications have become ever more important in the selection process. Since a judge's reelection to the highest bench is practically assured until he wishes to retire, his career assumes the characteristics of a civil service, as is customary in the rest of Western Europe.[34]

In the Soviet Union, the Bolshevik revolution abolished with one stroke the career judiciary of *its* ancien régime and replaced it with an elective system for all judgeships: those for the lower courts are elected directly, and the higher echelons are elected by the Soviets of the U.S.S.R. or of the Union Republics. But since candidates are nominated by the appropriate level of the party which never submits more than one candidate for each vacancy, the electoral process amounts to an endorsement of the party nominee. The party, however, consults the lawyers' association on the professional qualifications of available candidates so that, at least technically, the process bears considerable resemblance to the so-called bipartisan judicial elections in

[33] Danielski, 1969, pp. 55ff.

[34] Morrison, 1969, pp. 150ff.

American states. Now virtually all candidates for judicial appointment have a higher legal education, which was not the case even as late as 1936. Once elected a judge is theoretically not assured of any tenure, since those who elected him can also recall him. However, this appears to happen rarely. At the end of his term of office (uniformly one of five years) a judge's reelection is not automatic though reasons for the replacement of one candidate by another are seldom given. Nonetheless in the great majority of cases Soviet judges enter upon a judicial career at or near the beginning of their professional lives and are promoted from lower courts to higher courts on the basis of ability. This makes the judiciary something like a career service, differing from that of other civil-law countries only by the formal process of election.[35]

The Communist countries of Eastern Europe have abandoned only gradually their traditional pattern of a career judiciary. By now elections have become the general practice; yet they are always indirect, usually through the legislatures. Professional requirements, the study of law, and additional experience are the rule and are emphasized as much as they are now in the Soviet Union.

Except for the somewhat divergent case of Switzerland, all non-Communist European countries recruit their judges through a career service. The same situation obtains in Latin America and in most of the countries of Asia and Africa that have adopted the juridical structure of the civil-law world. After the required university courses and usually a prescribed practical training period, success in demanding examinations opens a life-time career which invariably starts at the lower echelons of the judicial hierarchy. Especially of late attempts have been made—for example, in Italy under pressure from its judiciary—to give to the judicial career some features distinguishing it from that of other civil servants. But by mentality as well as by background the European judge and the Latin American judge have been and remain civil servants who have little if any professional or other outside experience. In 1970 there were about 16,000 full-time professional judges in the Federal Republic of Germany (population 62 million), 8,000 in Italy (population 52 million), and approximately 4,000 in France (population 50 million). In Italy and France one-third of these are members of the *Parquet*, the prosecuting staff, which shares training and career with the judges.

It is quite significant that, notwithstanding the political upsurges which have shaken Germany, Italy, and France over the last half-century, a large percentage of presently active judges in these countries are the sons or daughters of judges, civil servants, or lawyers. This is by itself an important factor in creating and maintaining the homogeneity of the judiciary. Discreetness, anonymity, and a high degree of honesty and professionalism are the common characteristics of most continental judges, qualities which are

[35] Barry and Berman, 1971, pp. 307–8.

congruent with the features and the style of the judicial process (see below Chapters 5 and 6). A lack of mobility prevents the cross-fertilization which the American judge and English judge will generally derive from the variety of legal experiences that they have had before their appointment. Such exposure easily makes for a more forceful and resourceful personality than service in the same hierarchy which one has entered immediately upon the termination of one's training period. Even social contacts between a European judge and other jurists are none too frequent. This is different in the Soviet Union and in Yugoslavia where it is possible to move from a judgeship to activities as a jurisconsult or advocate and later be chosen for another judgeship.

The apparent advantage of the European pattern is the routine way of the initial appointment which when coupled (at least in all democracies) with tenure for life seems to guarantee judicial immunity against all interference. It is quite true that neither political pressures nor favoritism play a role at the time a successful candidate enters the career. The critical problem here is promotion, the more or less rapid advancement of judges to higher and more important posts. The mere fact that professional judgeships are far more numerous in Europe than in England or the United States makes concern for promotion a condition of judicial life.

For a long time decisions on promotion were exclusively in the hands of the government, acting usually through its Ministry of Justice or a comparable administration. It was a foregone conclusion that all regimes, whether liberal or authoritarian, would reward loyalty and conformism when possibilities for advancement opened up. While demotions were difficult, transfer to some uninteresting judgeship in the provinces was always a possibility.

At present the problem has not lost its acuity. For understandable reasons a concern that the power to promote might be wielded to interfere, albeit indirectly, with judicial independence has been particularly acute in post-totalitarian Italy and Germany. In ten years of intense struggle Italian judges have succeeded in wresting discretionary powers from the Ministry and in entrusting them to a High Council of the Magistrature in which judges have a clear majority and from which the Minister is altogether excluded. According to some observers the self-administration of the judiciary in Italy is now greater than in any other European country, especially since the Constitutional Court has declared unconstitutional a law which sought to restrict the powers of the High Council.[36]

Western Germany has sought to draw lessons from the period of the Weimar Republic when a reactionary judiciary sabotaged most effectively the institutions of the democratic state. Now there are procedures, at both the federal and the Land level, designed on the one hand to check too strict a control of the executive over promotions and other rewards and on the

[36] Moriondo (1966) 1969, pp. 312–15.

other to prevent the systematic hostility of the judiciary towards the state.

The regime of the French Fifth Republic has moved in an opposite direction by modifying provisions of the constitution of the Fourth Republic which gave to members of parliament and of the judiciary some control over appointments and promotions to higher positions. A reorganisation of the High Council of the Magistrature has vested once more and in only thinly disguised form all such powers in the political executive. For promotions that are not within the Council's purview, a young judge's advancement is decided by the "notations" which he receives from his elders and supervisors and which are communicated to him only in part. This opens the way to reward conformism and penalize independence. A serious degradation of morale through the judicial hierarchy has been one of the consequences.[37] Early in 1969 the official French judges' association complained stridently: "The authorities have continued to promote [judges] abusively . . . in fact access to high positions in the judiciary is granted with increasing frequency to judges whose lack of seniority is compensated by nothing except merits that have no relation with the way in which they have attended to their professional duties."[38]

If institutional or informal arrangements might, under the best of circumstances, reduce political influence over judges' careers, they are unable to eradicate some of the vices that are the reverse of the virtues of the European career service. Cautiousness, self-restraint, and possibly professional sycophancy appear to most judges as useful attitudes if they wish to move to more rewarding posts. This permits the continuing socialization of a majority of judges into roles that serve system maintenance more than other ends which the law and the judicial process ought to pursue.

This is one of the reasons why, unlike the situation in the United States, England, and the Commonwealth countries, many of the finest legal talents in civil-law countries do not aspire to a judicial post. In any society the profession of the private attorney comes among all law jobs closest to the free-enterprise model of self-selection. The requirements for professional qualifications set by the government, the professional associations, or both, may be more or less onerous. But once they are met, the attorney enters a "liberal" profession, bound, it is true, by canons of professional ethics, but not depending on any official approval of his activities or his juristic or political thinking. This explains why in many systems, but especially in the European setting, ethnic and religious minority groups still struggling for recognition have furnished a disproportionately high number of attorneys-at-law. And Lenin was not the only revolutionary who chose the law as a profession because it offered the best opportunities to pursue his extracurricular interests.

---

[37] Williams and Harrison, 1971, p. 270, and the bitter complaints by a Parisian judge: Casamayor, 1973b ("One does not pay the judges, one rewards them").

[38] *Le Monde*, June 12, 1969.

More recently one notices in several countries, and independently of the legal family to which the system may belong, a new type of attorney who by his activities and his announced principles wishes to alter the traditional role of the advocate.[39] This has led to what has been described above as the explosion of advocacy. No longer content to perform services for a client who can afford his fee, the new type of attorney is policy rather than client oriented. Where he tries to further particular causes and to achieve certain political goals by litigation, he transgresses the traditional bounds of the attorney-client relationship. But he thereby also introduces a new dimension into the legal culture within which he moves.

A parallel and connected development concerns the changes involving the professional organizations in a number of countries. The influence of these associations on training, selection, socialization, and, when necessary, disciplining the legal profession has been alluded to earlier in this study. The American Bar Association is probably one of the most powerful lawyers' organizations in the world. But these organizations play a considerable role in many countries. A study of legal culture should pay attention to them because their activities touch on many aspects of both the legal profession and legal life. As yet, however, no comparisons can be undertaken because even monographic treatments of the more important national associations, their membership, their influence, their ideologies, and other data that would lend themselves to comparison are lacking.

In several countries the organizations of the legal profession are losing their former more or less monolithic unity. Attorneys, and sometimes even judges, dissatisfied with their traditional role, have raised critical voices either as an opposition within the established associations or by forming their own organizations. One of the lasting innovations brought on by the May-June 1968 events in France has been the establishment of a unionlike organization of French judges, the *Syndicat de la Magistrature*, grouping more than one-fourth of the active judges of all grades. The competition from the *Syndicat* compelled the old established organization of French judges to change its structure and to take a more activist stand on questions pertaining to the status of judges. Since in many countries the opposition recruits principally among the younger members of the profession, questions of a generational conflict are undoubtedly of some importance. But this is not uniformly so. Most of these movements and groups publish journals and magazines discussing a wide range of professional questions and also issues of legal policy and new fields of law. The striking resemblance among these movements and their thinking in different countries is an indication that they are transgressing the boundaries of a given legal culture.

[39] For what follows in the text, see also Grossman and Sarat, 1971, p. 196, and the authors there quoted.

THE WAYS AND MEANS OF THE LAW I

5

CONFLICT RESOLUTION AND JUDICIAL PROCESS

There has been much praise for "preventive politics," the art of avoiding political conflicts so that there is no need to settle them, just as preventive medicine forestalls the need for healing and cure. Who will attend to that task—the legislature, the political executive, or the bureaucracy—will depend on the regime and on the situation in which preventive action is recognized as necessary. Where conflicts cannot (and sometimes should not) be avoided, the process of politics is counted on to keep them within manageable limits. Norms settling legal relations between man and man or between citizens and their community have a similar preventive function. Earlier anthropologists had described the behavior of men in primitive society as determined by the "cake of custom": where everybody knew the limits of acceptable behavior and where the price for transgressing them was intolerably high, legal machinery was all but unnecessary. More recent research has made it appear dubious whether this kind of self-enforced harsh harmony has ever prevailed for long in any culture. It is certain that a dynamic and developing society would not want to rely on this mode of conflict prevention.

On the other hand, even the most differentiated and specialized norms are not relied upon solely to settle disputes but, wherever possible, to obviate them. This explains the efforts to make rules as precise and adequate as possible so as to diminish uncertainties about respective rights and duties. Where the outcome of a dispute between contending parties appears evident, at least to "reasonable men," society may frequently be spared the cost of settlement in the public arena. When the maintenance of public order is disturbed by criminal behavior or other irrational motivations or when grave societal maladjustments make it difficult to avoid conflicts, there is still advantage in defining what is forbidden as clearly as possible and in announcing credible sanctions.

But because, just like preventive medicine, preventive law might not work, every society must provide means of conflict resolution. Given the wide variety of available methods for the settlement of disputes, it is remarkable that in some form most societies use similar methods. Differences consist rather in the preference given to one method over others. Cultural attitudes at least as much as available structures will usually determine such preferences.

Two major forms of resolving legal disputes are known the world over. *Either* the parties to a conflict determine the outcome themselves by negotiation, which does not preclude that a third party acting as a mediator might assist them in their negotiations. *Or,* the conflict is adjudicated, which means that a third, and ideally impartial, party decides which of the disputants has the superior claim. As will be shown both of these models can be used (and are sometimes intertwined) for the settlement of civil, criminal, and administrative suits. Where adjudicatory structures are scarce or where any kind of litigation is looked upon with disdain, settlement by negotiation will be the preferred solution. For this reason international conflicts are most effectively solved by direct negotiations between interested nation-states. For in spite of some appearances, institutions capable of enforcing a solution against the will of nation-states are still lacking. International society and its law resemble a primitive culture which has as yet developed neither appropriate structures nor the needed consensus for adjudicating conflicts and for enforcing decisions of third-party settlement. In the cultures of the Far East, not so much the absence of such structures but a reluctance to have recourse to them puts a high price on settlement by the parties with or without the help of a mediator.

Even in a society with a fully developed court system and other possibilities for adjudication, many disputes will never enter its judicial institutions nor be submitted to alternative procedures aimed at binding settlement by a third party.[1] The unavoidable (and not only material) costs of all formal proceedings and the often meager results of a court decision (to be discussed below, Chapter 7) will persuade a large number of disputants in all societies, both West and East, not to insist on their rights when settlement by negotiation has not been successful. Similarly the guardians of the public order, the prosecuting authorities, will make use of their wide discretion not to seek sanction for a violation of existing rules, however flagrant the violation may be.

Frequently the courts themselves will encourage disputants to settle by agreement since this is a less costly way to reestablish an equilibrium which

---

[1] See Abel, 1974, p. 228, for an excellent discussion of the relationship between dispute settlement and judicial institutions.

any conflict is likely to disturb. A settlement may be encouraged even after the parties have brought their complaint to a court or other tribunal. Such efforts may be undertaken by the judge in pretrial hearings or in open court. Whether they are successful will again depend not only on the talent of the judge or any arbitrator and on the nature of the conflict, but also on the value which cultural norms have attached to amicable agreement.

Similarly, even where a prosecuting authority has opened proceedings against an accused, settlement by negotiation is not precluded. When criminal suits in the United States are settled by plea-bargaining, this amounts to nothing else than an agreement "out of court" (to be discussed below). Methods used in dealing with criminal or asocial behavior in Communist China frequently have some of the same characteristics.

Where the parties are unable or unwilling to resolve their dispute by agreement and when they have decided against letting matters rest, formal adjudication must take over, and will end normally in a decision which claims to be binding on the parties, whoever they are, private or public.

Even where adjudication is resorted to, there are alternatives to judicial or court procedures; such alternatives are available and widely used in most legal systems at varied stages of development. (Some of them will be discussed below in Chapter 6.) Past experiences and cultural differences will frequently decide whether a case is submitted to the regular courts or to another adjudicating agency. Sometimes mere expediency is the controlling factor. One of the wisest American judges, Justice Learned Hand, once remarked: "as a litigant I should dread a law suit beyond almost anything else short of sickness and death." [2] Also in the most modern societies a law suit decided by the courts may be an inefficient, costly, and indeed "archaic" way of conflict settlement. Yet a relatively greater predictability of the outcome might make reliance on the court preferable to other procedures.

Litigiousness, the propensity to settle disputes through the judicial process, is undoubtedly a cultural factor of some significance. Authors who have attempted to compare such attitudes cross-culturally have found it convenient to measure them by an index of civil cases initiated per unit of population.[3] Although, with one exception, available figures refer only to developed societies, the accompanying table by Grossman and Sarat reveals in many ways wide and surprising variations.[4] Accurate though the raw data in this table might be, they should be refined considerably to provide reliable comparative explanation. As they stand they run counter to some widely held assumptions about the litigiousness of various nations. "In England 'the

---

[2] As quoted by Frank, 1956, p. 909.

[3] Grossman and Sarat, 1973, p. 2.

[4] Ibid., p. 26. The authors are the first to recognize this. Their carefully compiled figures demonstrate how little truly comparative data can be derived from statistical material.

Litigation Rates

Country or State	Civil cases per 100,000 population
Australia	5,277 (1969)
Denmark	4,844 (1969)
New Zealand	4,423 (1969)
Great Britain	3,605 (1969)
West Germany	2,085 (1969)
Massachusetts	1,814 (1971)
Japan	1,257 (1970)
Sweden	683 (1970)
Finland	493 (1970)
New Hampshire	345 (1971)
Norway	307 (1970)
South Korea	172 (1963)

law' plays a less important role than in almost any other western country," a well-informed sociological study has stated.[5] Yet the table shows an extraordinary high litigation rate for Great Britain, higher than that for Western Germany, whose population is frequently described as being addicted to solving conflicts by law suits. The enormous difference between the rate in Denmark and other Scandinavian countries is difficult to explain, especially since other statistics indicate that Norway has about three times as many lawyers as Denmark. And how can we reconcile the relatively high litigation rate for Japan with the often-stated fact that even in postwar Japan courts are still not a highly valued site for conflict resolution? Sufficiently complete and reliable data are lacking for the United States which Tocqueville described (see above, Chapter 3) as having a passion for law suits, and which has still by far the highest number of lawyers per capita. Differences shown in the table for two neighboring states, Massachusetts and New Hampshire, are startling; they point to the likely fact that the socioeconomic characteristics of a state or the particularities of its historic court system will have an effect on people's inclination to take their troubles to the courts. But why the difference between two New England states should be that enormous remains unexplained. A study of four Wisconsin cities has suggested that "political culture may be a significant explanatory device for accounting for differences in litigation rates" and that the choice to employ the courts for private purposes may be guided by "orientations toward public life as well as by public norms of what constitutes appropriate use of government facilities."[6] But available data do not permit one to go beyond such generalities.

[5] Abel-Smith and Stevens, 1967, p. 1.

[6] Quoted here from Grossman and Sarat, 1971, p. 185.

An interesting index of litigiousness would be one indicating the proportion between the total number of cases and those appealed to a higher court. But here again mere numbers would not reveal all of the pertinent facts. What would be even more informative would be a comparison between law suits and the total number of conflicts in several societies. If such an index could be constructed, which is improbable, it is apt to show not only regional discrepancies, but also great differences in the use of courts by different subcultures in a society. Appeal to the courts is obviously connected not only with individual motivations but also with the confidence placed by a certain population group in legal institutions. Not only in the United States but also elsewhere poor people are much less likely than the middle classes to perceive an advantage in taking their grievances to court. The question of cost is only one factor, and where legal aid is available it is not even the most important one that makes for such a difference. What has been shown for the United States is probably true everywhere: the legal system is inaccessible to the poor because neither they nor the system recognize the problems of the poor as legal problems.[7]

Some of the legal services programs in the United States have considered it their foremost task to break down the low opinion of the efficacy of litigation in the culture of the poor.[8] Our earlier discussion of new forms of advocacy (see above, Chapter 4) indicated that the growth of class actions, of test cases, and generally the use of litigation as a pressure-group tactic all try to overcome the strictly individualistic character of traditional court procedures.[9] It remains to be seen whether and to what extent this will change the lack of confidence in litigation felt by large segments of the public.

Significant differences exist in the scenario and style of court procedures and of judicial decision-making. (They will be discussed below and in Chapter 6). But certain important features of the judicial process and of legal reasoning are constant throughout so many legal cultures that one might conclude there is a "reasonable *a priori* case for the functional necessity of the procedure."[10]

A modicum of judicial impartiality and an obligation of the court to decide every case over which it has jurisdiction are connected aspects, and both are inherent in the function of rational court procedure. Unless the court shows an aura of objectivity when it sifts the evidence submitted by the parties, its decision will lack the respect that is indispensable for effective conflict resolution. What is at stake here is not the independence of the

---

[7] See Abel, 1974, p. 332, fn. 325.

[8] Ibid., p. 186. No comparative data could be uncovered.

[9] See Grossman and Sarat, 1973, p. 24.

[10] March (1956), 1964, p. 136.

judge from political authority (discussed above), but his independence from either party. In certain situations, the latter might be as nonexistent as the former. Yet most legal systems grant the parties the right to challenge the presence of judges, learned or lay, about whose impartiality there exist substantiated doubts.

However, once a court has taken a case under consideration, it has the duty to decide it. The Napoleonic code has formulated explicitly what is considered elsewhere as a general principle: no legal order can tolerate the denial of judgment by the competent judicial officer.[11] For such a denial would leave the unsettled conflict an open sore and this would, at least in principle, be equally intolerable for a civil and for a criminal suit. The reverse is also true: by supplying its decision whenever they are in demand, and by participating thereby in the policy output of the system, the judiciary preserves its own existence and its continuing role in society.

Another universal feature of the judicial process, at least in its contemporary forms, is that all judgments be derived from a norm.[12] Conflict settlement "out of court" can rely on considerations of what is equitable and good, on mere expediency, or on discretion. In actual fact, judicial settlement might use similar standards. But in order to acquire legitimacy, it must explain how its decision connects with a previously established norm. From this perspective judge and administrator have much in common, for it is indeed possible to view the judicial process as a specialized administrative process that the parties to a dispute have set in motion. In all systems the substance and existential validity of a norm are not enshrined in the text of a constitution or of a statute nor in the *ratio decidendi,* the reasoned decision, of a precedent. What the norm is will depend on the fate it suffers in the judicial or administrative process. That process, however, will in turn be determined at every turn by the cultural environment in which it operates. (For more details, see below, Chapter 6.)

SCENARIO OF JUDICIAL PROCEEDINGS

Every legal rule amounts to an "if—then" statement. The "if" is to be filled in by the kind of facts which the rule has designated as prerequisites for its application.[13] Courts, as well as other adjudicatory agencies, are committed to a search of the pertinent facts and in their search they will act as "historians" trying to reconstruct

---

[11] The text of article 4 provides: "An action for the denial of justice can be brought against a judge who refuses to give judgement in a case on the ground that the law is silent, obscure or incomplete." Recently a commission charged with revising the French Civil Code has recommended the elimination of this provision as unnecessary because self-evident.

[12] See, also for what follows, Kirchheimer, 1961, p. 179.

[13] Frank, 1956, p. 898.

past events as best as they can. As in any such search the available evidence must be sifted and evaluated. While this process necessarily allows for a large amount of discretion, every legal system has its rules which prescribe or at least recommend how the historian-judge should go about his task. Where procedures differ, almost identical legal norms might in their application lead to different results.

This is easily understood when one compares the treatment of criminal behavior in democratic and totalitarian countries. The wording of certain provisions of the criminal law can be almost identical. Yet, especially when the incriminated behavior has political overtones, the disposition of the case may be drastically different in the two systems. But differences in procedures will also affect judicial decisions in common-law and civil-law countries, although under the impact of similar economic and technological developments, substantive norms have often become alike. Legal thought and legal life are moving in tracks laid out by procedures, many of which have been inherited from a more or less distant past. "Whenever," Oliver Wendell Holmes wrote in 1881, "we trace a leading doctrine of substantive law far enough back, we are very likely to find some forgotten circumstance of procedure at its source." [14] Without being able to seek out their historical roots a comparative study of contemporary systems must still explain the various methods of fact-finding employed by the courts, civil as well as criminal.

At least in modern times the investigation of relevant facts will start well ahead of the trial, which is usually public. Unavoidably, the structure of the trial and especially the role assigned by the system to judges and parties will shape pretrial procedures just as the outcome of the latter will mark the trial itself. The most significant difference between the situation in common-law and in civil-law countries results from the fact that in the former the days in court are far more of an event than in systems of the Romano-Germanic family. This is clearly the consequence of the greater importance attributed to the participation of the jury in the Anglo-American tradition. When the facts must be viewed by a jury, which is assembled in court for this purpose, they must be concentrated and their significance must be heightened to the point of dramatization. Where this is not the case and where trial procedures can be permitted to become a sequence of detached fragments rather than a unified courtroom drama, the preparation will cover more ground. Facts will be sifted without the concern prevalent in Anglo-American procedures that the preparation should not fix a picture of the situation in the judge's mind before the trial has begun. As will be discussed below, everywhere jury trials have lost much of their importance in civil matters, and in England this is also true of criminal proceedings.

[14] Holmes, 1881, p. 253.

Yet this has not altered some of the basic features which were attuned to the need of presenting the facts to a body of lay judges.

Widely heralded differences in the preparation of a criminal trial are actually the basis for one of the major controversies about the respective virtues of common-law and civil-law systems. The designation of the former as "accusatorial" and of the latter as "inquisitorial" is misleading, though it does point to differences in their historical origins and in their fundamental assumptions concerning the ends and means of punishment.[15] Since the eighteenth century, the development of the continental system has been a deliberate move away from criminal justice based on private vengeance. The role of the private accuser was taken over by public officials who were free to seek out the evidence which in their eyes could prove useful to the ends of their inquiry. By putting an end to the secrecy and to the essentially written form of that inquiry, the French Revolution deprived criminal procedures of their dangerously oppressive features.

By contrast the common-law system has far longer relied on a private accuser and thereby conserved also to the criminal trial the characteristics of adversary proceedings. Their traditional model remained the duel fought before an impartial arbiter, the judge, and the defendant's peers, the jury. The development of a public prosecutor and a professional police force to investigate suspected crimes is a relatively recent development in common-law countries and a step away from the accusatorial towards the inquisitorial system.

Contrary to an erroneous but frequently encountered opinion, both systems assume the innocence of the accused until his guilt has been proven. The French Declaration of the Rights of Man solemnly pronounced this principle in 1789. The question rather seems to be whether the conduct of the pretrial investigation and the scenario of the trial itself are under certain circumstances so heavily loaded against the defendant that the assumption of innocence is totally or partially defeated. In England and the United States "honest countrymen," the grand juries, were looked upon as a protection against overeager criminal prosecution. (Whether they have fulfilled this role will be discussed below.) A European and Latin American institution which is officially praised as serving the ends of an efficient yet fair investigation is unknown to common-law systems. The *juge d'instruction* or *Untersuchungsrichter* is a member of the judiciary who examines the material submitted by the police or by private persons and who advises the prosecuting authorities whether or not criminal proceedings are warranted. The role of this investigating magistrate is frequently described as shielding the suspect from his "natural enemy" the prosecutor who is always willing to haul persons into court and to win a case so as to further his own career. (It is well

---

[15] See, also for what follows, Merryman, 1969, pp. 135ff.

known that in the United States the office of the district attorney is highly politicized. But the same situation may prevail elsewhere.)

To fulfill his assigned role, the *juge d'instruction* should be totally independent and able to ward off any pressures from whatever side they may come. This, however, is not always, and in the opinion of some close observers, only rarely the case. In many countries the examining magistrate is in close touch with the prosecution and especially with the police to whom he might and frequently must delegate parts of the investigation. The extensive interrogation to which the judge can submit the accused in his chambers will often prove more hazardous to the suspect than an encounter with the judge in England and the United States where he needs only to announce how he will plead. Particularly strident complaints have been voiced in France where until recently the defense attorney was denied access to the files during the pretrial investigative phase.[16]

It is true that the examining magistrate will never make a final determination of guilt and will tender only advice to the prosecuting authorities. Yet "the form he has given to his inquiry tends to shape the proceedings in court and often tips the balance in case of doubt." [17] To this it must be added that in most civil-law countries those accused of all but trivial offenses are likely to spend the often lengthy period of investigation in jail. All it takes to keep them there is a decision that their detention is necessary "for the discovery of the truth." An official hostility towards the institution of bail is often motivated by noble egalitarian rationalizations: where criminal behavior is involved questions of money should not enter since this would favor the wealthy over the poor. Tragedies resulting from the protective custody of innocent and guilty alike are frequent in Europe. Only in very recent times has legislation been introduced in some countries, and France foremost among them, to generalize American and British practice. Yet as late as 1973, 45 percent of the French prison population were people awaiting trial.

But the question of the relative justice of the two systems can only be answered after an examination of the actual trial stage. Before turning to a consideration of that stage it must be emphasized that the actual outcome of most criminal trials, and possibly of many other suits as well, may depend largely on the role which the police authority plays not only in the preparation of the trial but also throughout the trial itself. In all modern societies the police force is an integral part of the legal culture, no less than are judges and other "officers of the law." Its methods and its integration and relation-

---

[16] For a critical (and some would say overcritical) discussion of the situation by a French judge, see Casamayor, 1970, pp. 113ff.

[17] Fuller, 1961, p. 36. Most of this article is devoted to an excellent comparative discussion.

ship with other parts of the judicial and administrative apparatus depend on the political and legal traditions of the system which it serves. At least in a democracy the police cannot help but become the focus for clashes between frequently conflicting values: that of protecting the individual and his legitimate interests and that of assisting the effective attainment of a public purpose such as law and order.

Not only in a police state or in other authoritarian systems, but everywhere is the police force endowed with a considerable amount of factual discretion. This may lead to an arbitrary use of power and to a readiness on the part of the police to take the law into their own hands. The professionalization of the police force, its involvement in or its distance from the community with which it interacts, the esteem or the disdain in which the police force is held, and the different uses to which various branches of the police are put in a given system—all these are relevant factors for the evaluation of a legal culture. The insights to be gained from a comparative treatment would be considerable. Such an investigation must lift many a curtain made of appearances and pretensions. To give but one example: it is not realistic to expect that in the United States a Supreme Court decision prescribing norms for the interrogation of suspects will change the actual proceedings in many thousands of police stations throughout the country (on this point also see below, Chapter 7). However, for reasons of space a discussion of the role of the police in the legal life of modern societies must be reserved for a separate treatment.[18]

At the trial stage variations between the assumptions underlying the common-law and the civil-law systems emerge most clearly. This is true in both civil and criminal matters. Starting from different models of proceedings the dissimilarities between Anglo-American and continental methods of evidence-gathering have remained until today "important, and in some respects, spectacular."[19] An unusually well-informed American judge has concluded from looking at both systems that the "mode of trial seriously affects the manner in which substantive legal rules work in various countries" and that "burden of proof rules may completely sterilize substantive rules."[20]

In the adversary system of the common law the discovery of the "truth," that is, of the facts at dispute, is essentially left to the parties. The judge's traditional role has been that of a referee or an impartial arbiter who decides what line of questioning and which materials are allowed to enter the minds of the jury. This seemingly liberal model of conflict and of conflict resolution is based on an implied premise of equality between the two parties. In fact

---

[18] For a comparative discussion, see Chapman, 1970; also very useful is Bordua, 1968, pp. 174–81, and the sensitive essay by Casamayor, 1973a.

[19] Friedmann, 1967, p. 531.

[20] Frank, 1956, p. 897.

the notion, foreign to civil-law countries, that law is a game of skills with handicaps so arranged that the most skillful side has a better chance to win even if his case might be weaker, works to the advantage of the party that is represented by the more talented counsel.[21] But talent, resources for preparation, and the respectability of counsel are expensive items which, even in a civil suit, might not be equally distributed. When prosecutor and defendant face each other in a criminal trial, equality might be even more fictitious, even though the court will see to it that the game is played according to rules and not turn "dirty." Such common-law rules as the "best evidence," the "best witness," or the exclusion of hearsay (all unknown rules in civil-law systems) sometimes appear as a hindrance to the discovery of the truth. They are motivated by a constant and frequently quite realistic concern that the court (judges and jury alike) should be prevented from being swayed emotionally by too many raw facts.

Even today the role of the Anglo-American judge, especially in courts of lower instance, is easily assimilable to that of a father or a neighbor helping the feuding parties in their troubles. A distinctly educational and moralistic tone might pervade the courtroom and all participants are, at least indirectly, admonished to play their part in such a scenario. It is quite in line with the judge's role as a father figure, stern or benign as the circumstances require, that he can enforce respect for his presence and his decisions by far more efficient contempt powers than those available to his brethren in civil-law systems.[22]

The Scandinavian countries, and especially Sweden, were described earlier as standing midway between the two systems. This is quite striking in regard to court procedures. Fact-finding techniques and rules of evidence are similar to those of other European countries. But especially under the influence of postwar legislation the role of the judge has become more and more that of a fatherly umpire of the parties who do not even need to be represented by counsel.

How active or passive a part the judge may play in the adversary system has been a frequent subject of dispute. One of the system's main assets, the participation of the parties in fact-finding, will be more valuable, especially in a complicated modern society, when the judge has set a frame for the contest and possibly even disclosed what he considers important facts to be elucidated.[23] Expressing his impatience with some of the delays and inequities of the adversary systems, a U.S. Supreme Court Justice has stated (in a dissenting opinion): "Federal judges are not referees at prize fights, but

[21] For a more comprehensive development of these points, see Kirchheimer, 1961, pp. 342ff.

[22] See Pekelis, 1950, pp. 45–53, for a comparative treatment of this question.

[23] Fuller, 1961, p. 41.

functionaries of justice." [24] Such a characterization corresponds entirely to the image of the judge in civil-law countries.

In civil-law countries the judge is expected to direct the proceedings on his own in such a way that the truth emerges. He may do so with the help of the parties where this is possible. But he may also, and in quite authoritarian fashion, use methods that both parties scorn because they may lead to the uncovering of facts that are harmful to their interests. The civil-law judge considers himself to be secure and rational enough to hear, gather, and evaluate whatever evidence is or becomes available. He will not exclude hearsay but will decide what probative value is to be given to it. If necessary, he will not hesitate to use forceful language to open the eyes of the jurors to what appears to him as possible distortions of facts. (What impact this had on the jury trial will be discussed below.) It is true that in many instances this description of an activist judge might appear exaggerated. Temper and temperament will determine his actual role. He can also be as passive as he wishes to be. At every stage of a trial a civil-law judge is free to examine all documentary evidence; this cannot always be done in American trials and has only recently been made possible in England. He can by his own initiative call for expert witnesses of his choosing and request them to shed light on facts he wishes to see elucidated. This privilege assumes particular importance since under modern conditions there is normally in many trials increasing reliance on expert evidence in place of lay testimony. Experts frequently become assimilated to the body of officials within the court.[25] But if this is the case there is advantage in having the judge rather than the parties decide on the desirability of their testimony.

Because of his pivotal position the civil-law judge will seldom even make the pretense that he enters the courtroom with an empty mind concerning the issues of the case before him. Instead, he has studied the files with care and may even have come close to reaching his decision. In spite of the principle of oral hearings, written procedures prevail at least in civil matters and might amount to an extensive exchange of briefs by legal experts. To be sure, this is not tolerated in criminal proceedings, but the possibility cannot be avoided that here too the judge has preconceived opinions and is influenced by the views of police and prosecutor.

Proceedings organized in this way, with much evidence submitted in writing and a good part of the interrogation of the parties conducted by the judge, leave little room for cross-examination, which is considered in common-law countries the most effective way of getting at the truth. Actually European and Latin American attorneys and prosecutors are little versed in this fine art. Moreover, since a criminal defendant in these countries is

---

[24] Justice Frankfurter in Johnson v. United States, 333 U.S. 46, 54 (1948) (emphasis supplied).

[25] See Abel, 1974, p. 276.

never obligated to take the stand in his own case, one misses out on his cross-examination, frequently a highlight in an Anglo-American trial. But to criticize the so-called inquisitorial system because it does not protect the accused against self-incrimination in the manner of the Fifth Amendment amounts to cultural ethnocentricity. In civil-law countries the defendant can choose whether or not he wishes to make a statement, usually designated as "the last word." Since such a statement will never be under oath, he can say what he wants, and what he says will be evaluated freely like all other evidence. On the other hand the American defendant is often confronted with the dilemma of either perjuring himself or, by his refusal to testify, destroying his credibility especially in the eyes of the jurors.[26]

In comparing the two systems in terms of their final outcome for the accused, the evaluation of a life-long observer of both has been quoted.[27] If he were innocent, he said, he would prefer to be tried by a civil-law court, but if he were guilty, he thought his chances for escaping or mitigating punishment were better before a common-law court. In many cases this is undoubtedly true. It suggests that criminal proceedings in civil-law countries are apt to distinguish more accurately between the guilty and the innocent. However, what was said earlier about the importance of police procedures must always be kept in mind.

The Anglo-American criminal trial is based on the assumption of a happy equilibrium between the prosecutor and the accused. But there is probably no system in the world where such an equilibrium exists. How heavily the imbalance weighs in the final outcome will easily depend on the special circumstances of the case and the general setting which the system provides for criminal trials. In many instances it will be even more important how much the judge and jury are impressed by the fact that the prosecution represents the authority of the state, while even under the best of circumstances the defense attorney fights for the rights of an individual under suspicion. The more authoritarian the society, the higher the prestige of the prosecution, and the more limited that of his counterpart. In a totalitarian or even authoritarian country, the arguments of the defense are sometimes deliberately weak, especially where the imputed felony is presented as an attack against the fundamental tenets of the state.[28]

Court proceedings in the Soviet Union follow in general the civil-law

26 The issue was discussed in comparative terms in United States v. Grunewald 233 F, 2d, 556 (1956), reprinted in Schlesinger, 1959, pp. 13ff.

27 By Merryman, 1969, p. 139.

28 For the humiliating status of the defense attorney in the German Democratic Republic (East Germany), see Kirchheimer, 1961, p. 275. For the situation in the Soviet Union, Feifer, 1964, reports (p. 283 and passim) that, at least in the early sixties, defense attorneys were given the possibility of doing a conscientious job. This was certainly not the case during the period on which Solzhenitsyn reports.

pattern. But since the educational function of the law and of all judicial proceedings is heavily stressed there are certain quite remarkable parallels between the position of the American and the Soviet judge. In the field of
criminal procedures the Soviet Union has made an original contribution
embedded more in general views on the function of the law than in specifically socialist ideologies. In all criminal trials the prosecutor may be assisted by a "community accuser," the *obshchestvennost,* who as foreman at
the defendant's place of work, or as a kolkhoz official, or as a trade-union
delegate and the like has known the defendant and his milieu. Where he
participates in the proceedings (in about one-tenth of all criminal cases) he
may recommend either a harsher or a more lenient penalty than that suggested by prosecution or defense. His pleadings will always be based on an
evaluation of the prisoner as a "whole man." His role is primarily that of
a mediator between the claims of the state authorities and community feelings.[29] Functionally his activities can be likened to those of a social worker
in American criminal trials.

As discussed before, Communist China has not seen fit to follow the
example of post-Stalinist Russia, which has stressed the advantages of legal
stability and predictability. The Mao regime has functioned without a
criminal code ever since gaining power. Its criminal proceedings aim at
speedy and efficient crime control and respect for due process is slighted.[30]
While the conclusions of the police are in most cases reviewed by the
prosecution and the courts, all three agencies operate in an informal, secret,
and inquisitorial manner. If and when the criminal process is invoked, in
ordinary as well as in political cases, the defendant is left with as little or
less procedural protection than was accorded to him in Stalinist Russia. On
the other hand Chinese Communists, in line with their general outlook on
the limited usefulness of law, apply criminal proceedings more sparingly.
Instead of a trial, use is made of persuasion, ideological incentives, and a
broad scale of social and administrative pressures applied wherever possible on a local and hence decentralized level.[31]

In the United States and in Great Britain the practice of "plea-bargaining" in criminal proceedings can be likened to a somewhat similar
settlement out of court. It too amounts to a radical departure from the
due-process model of crime control. An estimated 90 percent of all criminal
convictions in the United States are the result of plea-bargaining. What is involved here is different from a fairly universal occurrence, namely, a defendant's decision to confess rather than to deny guilt in order to move the
court to greater indulgence and possibly a lighter sentence. Instead, plea-
bargaining, normally undertaken by the prosecutor and the defense attorney,

[29] Feifer, 1964, pp. 280ff.

[30] See Packer, 1964, pp. 9–10 and 14–15.

[31] Cohen, 1968, pp. 48–53 and 123.

persuades the defendant more or less gently to plead guilty to a lesser crime or misdemeanor than the one he is charged with and of which he may or may not be guilty. By such a reduction of the charge he usually can avoid altogether a trial by jury which might have resulted in heavier punishment. In the process the prosecutor becomes the "dispute settler" and the manager of a ritualized conflict-resolution ceremony.[32] While this method of settlement is known primarily in countries committed to the adversary system of court proceedings, it completely perverts the assumptions of that system and turns it into one of administrative accommodation: prosecution and defense become friendly partners rather than adversaries; the defense attorney assumes the role of a coach preparing his client for meeting acceptable standards of behavior. The agreement prepared by the two sides is then submitted to the court for ratification. But at least in the United States, the judge might long before have stepped out of his presumably passive role and have pointed out to the defendant where his "real" interests lie.[33]

As a matter of fact, the practice, a clear violation of due process, is a direct outcome of the adversary system. Because of its slowness and costliness and also because of the comparatively small number of judges in the United States and Commonwealth countries, criminal justice would literally collapse without the extensive use of plea-bargaining. That the practice is extended to the misbehavior of the wealthy and the powerful has become widely known during the scandals surrounding the Nixon administration. But it is generally admitted that the poor and the low fare worst in this system. The pressure brought on them to plead guilty because their status or their past arouse suspicion results not infrequently in confessions of guilt by the innocent. One must conclude that conflict settlement by plea-bargaining, while seemingly serving the *administration* of justice, almost invariably betrays the cause of justice.

LAY PARTICIPATION IN THE JUDICIAL PROCESS	*In the judgement of offenses against the state the people ought to participate, for when any one wrongs the state all are wronged and may reasonably complain if they are not allowed to share in the decision. . . . And in private suits too, as far as possible, all should have a share, for he who has no share in the administration of*

justice is apt to imagine that he has no share in the state at all.[34]

The mixture of legal and political arguments which Plato presents in this passage in defense of lay participation in the judicial process is typical

---

[32] See Newman, 1966, Alschuler, 1968, and Casper, 1972.

[33] In England, where the practice is widespread too, there seems to be more concern for not involving the judge in any deals. For plea-bargaining in Great Britain generally, see Jackson, 1971, pp. 163–71.

[34] Plato, (350 B.C.) 1961, 767.

of the historical discussion of the problem, at least in the Western world. Since antiquity the desire to have citizens who are untrained in the law take a more or less prominent part in judicial proceedings grew out of a feeling that this opened a way for accommodating broad ethical maxims and legal reasoning. When the trial by witnessing neighbors (rather than by "peers" as it is often put) originated in England it replaced the crude and at times cruel ordeals, such as trial by oracles, wager combats, and the like, which had been used for the "judicial" settlement of conflicts. It is true that the verdict by twelve good and law-abiding men from the vicinity of the accused was not entirely unlike consulting an oracle. The general verdict by which today's jurors express their opinions about guilt or innocence without indicating the grounds for their decision has, because of its inscrutability, not entirely shed that oracular quality.

In a dynamic society such as the American colonies the jury verdict used in civil as well as criminal cases had a twofold advantage: it decided certain concrete issues of the law under the guise of finding the facts and it did so without creating binding precedents since no reasons for the decision needed to be given. Hence both flexibility and reliance on community judgment were furthered. The incorporation of the right to a jury trial into the Bill of Rights and most state constitutions was the natural consequence. At a time when dissatisfaction with some features of the jury trial led in England to a greater control by the judge over the jury, the American pioneer society gave vent to its bias against effective law enforcement by making, wherever possible, the jury into a counterweight to the suspected trial judge. When Tocqueville visited these shores and later wrote about his impressions, he was very enthusiastic about the widespread use of the jury in civil trials:

> When . . . the jury also acts on civil causes, its application is constantly visible; it affects all the interests of the community; everyone cooperates in its works: it thus penetrates into all the usages of life, it fashions the human mind to its peculiar forms, and is gradually associated with the idea of justice itself. . . . [the jury] imbues all classes with a respect for the things judged and with the notion of right.[35]

To Tocqueville and to others jury duty appeared as an excellent form of cultural and political socialization; it seemed to be particularly suited to a decentralized system of government which puts a premium on channeled citizen participation rather than on expressions of unbound direct democracy.

The United States has remained the mainstay of the classical jury trial, where a body of laymen reaches its decision on the facts of the case sepa-

---

[35] Tocqueville (1835), 1957, vol. 2, p. 295.

rately from the judge who is otherwise in control of the proceedings. It has been estimated that at present not less than 90 percent of all criminal jury trials the world over, and with very few exceptions all trials before a civil jury, are taking place in the United States. In any year approximately one million American jurors serve in some 100,000 criminal cases.[36] In England, the motherland of the jury, the right to jury trial in civil cases has been steadily restricted by decisions of either Parliament or the courts. The types of civil cases in which either side can insist on a jury trial—most of them with some kind of criminal flavor—are relatively rare and the actual use made of a jury in such cases is even more insignificant.[37] There is just little confidence left in the effectiveness of the participation of a jury in civil cases, even where the award of damages is at stake. The opinion of the prominent American judge Oliver Wendell Holmes that the laymen's evaluation of cause and standards of care in tort actions was precious, is not shared in present-day England and especially not by its highly professionalized judiciary.

Another once-revered Anglo-Saxon institution, the grand jury, was altogether abolished in England in 1933 and its disappearance has not been regretted. As originally conceived, the grand jury, composed of twenty-three men of substantial position, was to be a shield against capricious or otherwise unwarranted prosecution. The members of the grand jury heard as much of the evidence for the prosecution as they wished before deciding, after secret deliberation, whether the accused ought to be tried or not. The civil-libertarian features of the institution appealed to Jefferson and Madison who therefore made indictment by a grand jury one of the conditions for criminal prosecution before the federal courts. When trust in the fairness of the preliminary inquiries by English judges grew, it was felt, that the time-consuming and costly procedure of the grand jury added little to the protection of the rights of the accused and could therefore be dispensed with.

In the United States about half of the states still have recourse to the grand jury, and its use on the federal level remains constitutionally guaranteed. The benefits to be derived from the institution are highly controversial. Until 1968 when reforms were introduced by legislation, the composition of grand juries was particularly unrepresentative: a special mode of selection guaranteed that only middle-class white men, likely to enjoy each other's company as members of a Rotary Club might do, were serving on grand juries. There are substantiated claims that many grand juries have been little more than a rubber stamp for prosecutors and the F.B.I. They are frequently amenable to outbursts of public hysteria and have ridden rough-shod over the rights of accused and of witnesses. Not infrequently the U.S. Department of

---

[36] Abraham, 1968, p. 113.

[37] Jackson, 1967, pp. 72ff., for an up-to-date discussion of the use of the jury in England.

Justice relies on grand juries to uncover and extract evidence where the police have been unable or unwilling to go "far enough." Another observer, while admitting that the grand jury may well be "cumbersome, amateurish, time-consuming, annoying, emotional and a fifth wheel in the legal process," still believes that it serves "as a potentially powerful arm of direct democracy." [38] Until now the composition of the grand juries seems to have resulted at best in a severely filtered kind of direct democracy. Yet the role which various federal grand juries have played in the indictment of Nixon's staff and its henchmen has undoubtedly greatly increased the popularity of the institution.

In common-law countries the so-called petty jury remains an important feature of all criminal proceedings which might entail less than trivial punishment. Its essential function has been restated quite recently by the U.S. Supreme Court as "the interposition between the accused and his accusers of the common sense judgment of a group of laymen." [39] But continued and still widespread use of an age-old institution, surrounded by sentiment and emotion, is not tantamount to universal praise. The assumed assets or liabilities of the jury trial have been the subject of some of the most spirited and searching if inconclusive legal discussions. It is outside the framework of this study to adequately summarize and even less to evaluate the validity of the arguments put forward by admirers and critics. [40] The fact that trial by jury has maintained most of its historical forms only in common-law countries while it has withered or at least been thoroughly transformed elsewhere, is a consequence of those essential and culture-bound differences in the form of court proceedings which have been discussed earlier. The so-called adversary proceedings, costly and slow as they might be, made the role of the jury more meaningful and its shortcomings more tolerable: most of the time, the men and women in the jury box are at least able to obtain a coherent picture of the events surrounding the commission of the crime. This does not preclude the frequent irrationality of "jury-made law" from which the accused and the prosecution might seek escape by engaging in plea-bargaining. But where the case is settled by jury trial the latter's shortcomings are accepted as the price to be paid for conserving a way of legal life which it would be frivolous to discard altogether.

If many of the beliefs in the benefits of the jury trial have been demonstrated as being largely mythical, the myth has not lost its persuasive

---

[38] Abraham, 1968, p. 111. For a sharply critical view, see Cowan, 1973, pp. 19ff.

[39] Williams v. Florida, 399 U.S. 100, 78 (1970).

[40] Some of the most fundamental criticism of the jury system has come from an American appellate judge, Frank (1930), 1963, pp. 183–99 and 327–35. For an elaborate and on the whole favorable study of the workings of the jury in the United States, see Kalven and Zeisel, 1966. For a good critical and comparative discussion, see Becker, 1970, pp. 304–44.

strength. If, in the words of a British solicitor and law professor, "the traditional ideas of the jury as a safeguard of the liberty of the subject had been decently buried," [41] there are many judges as well as laymen who keep the "traditional ideas" alive. Incremental changes of the rules controlling jury trials have been introduced—in England by legislation, in the United States mostly by judicial review—whereas in civil-law countries attempts at reforming the jury system have been abandoned in favor of a thorough overhaul of criminal proceedings.

The democratic legitimation of the jury trial is intimately tied to the processes of selecting the jurors and to the social composition of the empaneled jurymen. Already in ancient Rome the establishment of the jurors' lists was the object of bitter class conflict. Wherever in modern Europe trial by jury was tried (see below), the working class found that it was invariably excluded from jury duty.[42] Also in the United States and England juries have seldom been truly representative of the population at large and hence were never, as the myth went, "a fair sampling of all one's neighbors." Instead most American state legislatures have found ways of guaranteeing that men of "middle rank," those whom Blackstone considered the "best investigators of truth, the surest guardians of public interest," outnumber those of lower status and education. Racial and ethnic minorities of whatever kind, as well as women, were constantly underrepresented. During recent decades decisions by federal and state courts have begun to remedy this situation as they have established minimal guidelines to ensure a greater representativeness of available panels.

But altering the composition of juries has led to new difficulties. As long as the jurors came largely from the same milieu, stubborn disagreements between the twelve men or women were relatively infrequent. Although the process of arriving at a verdict is an inviolable mystery which cannot be penetrated, it has often been maintained that quite frequently the best educated among the jurors would impose their views, and that for this reason alone a discrepancy of opinion between judges and jurors remained within reasonable bounds. Once the social homogeneity of the jurors is no longer guaranteed, a unanimous verdict becomes increasingly difficult to reach. The requirement that any verdict by the jury should be unanimous was based on the noble principle that as long as the twelve jurors did not agree there was reasonable doubt of the defendant's guilt, and also that it would take their accord to acquit convincingly. But now that disagreement and deadlock have become more frequent, the number of hung juries threatens to make the jury trial even more ponderous.

The British Criminal Justice Bill of 1967 permitted majority verdicts,

[41] Jackson, 1967, p. 304.

[42] See Weber (1922), 1954, p. 318.

but within strict limits: only one dissenting vote can be ignored for either acquittal or conviction. An increasing number of American states have gone farther in declaring that various forms of majority agreement on the verdict would be sufficient. A divided Supreme Court has found it necessary to sustain the constitutionality of such reforms, although so far the ruling applies only to state and not to the federal courts.[43] The impassioned concurring and dissenting opinions offered by the Justices in which they accuse each other of nothing less than being impervious to reality, betray fundamentally different conceptions about what is going on during jury deliberations.

To the exasperated libertarian on the court, Justice Douglas, to relax the requirement of a unanimous verdict was tantamount to abandoning the presumption of innocence. But the point could also be made that if under prevailing conditions no deviation from traditional requirements was permitted, the institution of the jury trial as such might not be able to survive. It can now be expected that the practice of requiring less than unanimity for conviction and acquittal will spread to more and more states. Since this could easily lead to overruling the votes of those minorities which have started to be selected for jury duty, the representativeness of jury verdicts could be challenged anew.

Among legal imports, the transfer of institutions and norms from one culture to another, trial by jury occupies a special place. The French philosophers had expressed their admiration for the openness of the English jury procedures and had praised them for their stark contrast to the secret and inquisitorial criminal trials of the continental monarchies. The demand for introducing trial by jury found its way into the *Cahiers* of 1789, and it would be a recurrent theme in all European bourgeois revolutions of the nineteenth century. Their participation in criminal proceedings was for the rising middle classes another weapon in their fight against aristocracy, professional judiciary, and an overpowering executive. Napoleon was able to count on jury trials to imprison his royalist opponents; his agents, it is true, were compiling the lists from which trustworthy jurors were to be selected.[44] The grand jury introduced at the time of the Revolution was soon abolished and its functions assumed once more by the prosecutor.

From France the criminal jury trial spread to most of the civil-law countries. (It was never extended to civil matters, Tocqueville's enthusiasm notwithstanding.) Even czarist Russia and Imperial Japan were able to accommodate a modified version, characterized by a tight supervision of the selection of reliable jurymen and the exclusion of all political felonies

---

[43] See Johnson v. Louisiana, 406 U.S. 356 (1972), and Apodaca, Cooper, and Madden v. Oregon, 406 U.S. 380–404 (1972).

[44] Seagle, 1932, p. 498.

from the right to a jury trial. Yet at present the pristine jury system in which a body of laymen finds independently and bindingly on the guilt or innocence of the accused has all but disappeared outside of the common-law world; the exceptions are a few small European democracies such as Austria, Norway, Belgium, and some of the Swiss cantons.[45]

In most countries experiences with the jury trial proved disappointing. A reform from which much had been expected turned out to be neither a "school for democracy" nor a "bulwark against oppression." The jury trial was ill-suited to criminal proceedings in civil-law systems. The inquisitorial form of the trial (see above), the importance of its preparatory phase, the domineering position of the professional magistrates and especially of the presiding judge were all apt to blur the evidence to the laymen. The differentiation between juries as triers of facts and judges as expositers of the law became altogether untenable in a changed procedural setting. (It is frequently criticized also in common-law countries and quite properly considered as a reflection of inherited cultural norms.[46]) In their predicament European jurors felt in need of advice from the bench, and such advice was given to them in forms which would be totally inadmissible in an Anglo-American jury trial. When they did not accept professional judgment, the jurors' verdicts were frequently, and especially in regard to certain crimes, eruptions of sheer emotionalism resulting in ludicrous convictions or acquittals. This in turn could only harden the authoritarian contempt of many of the career judges for this form of lay participation. Since in most countries workers were even more systematically excluded from jury duty than in England and the United States, the European labor movement showed little interest in defending the institution in its classical form.

At various periods the Weimar Republic, the Vichy Regime, and Mussolini abolished the jury trial by executive decree. When after the war democracy was reestablished in these countries and when their governments sought appropriate means of strengthening civic responsibility, the jury trial was not resurrected. European countries which are known for highly developed forms of participatory democracy, such as Sweden and the Swiss Confederation, have never introduced it. The sum total of these experiences demonstrates quite clearly that established legal traditions may preserve their influence even where there is intended or actual confluence of political goals.

The "mixed bench" common to many contemporary European systems, both East and West, can be considered as the functional equivalent of the jury trial. It fuses lay members and professional judges into a single body

[45] Casper and Zeisel, 1972, p. 135.

[46] Grossman and Sarat, 1971, p. 190.

finding on facts as well as on law and determining guilt and punishment in a single verdict. The mixed bench has some antecedents in old Germanic institutions antedating the introduction of the Anglo-American model on the continent. Its fairly successful performance might rather be due, however, to the way in which it combines desirable, yet controlled, lay participation with deference to the authority of the professional judiciary. To involve the laymen in the judicial process facilitates the input of popular values and sentiments and legitimizes not only the judicial output but the legal system itself. But from the beginning to the end of the trial the European "jurors" will receive the freely given advice of the usually forceful judge who will not hesitate to point out what he might consider errors in judgment or extravagances on the part of his untrained partners. The laymen in turn are free to communicate all through the trial with the outside world and hence to be in touch with the milieu from which they hail.

Obviously, this creates in the courtroom and especially in the chambers where the learned and the lay members of the bench deliberate together, a different atmosphere from that prevailing in a common-law jury trial. There are many variations in the composition and the modes of operation of such courts, differences not only between countries but also, as for instance in Sweden, between urban and rural regions and, elsewhere, differences according to the gravity of the offense. Different also is the weight given to the votes by laymen and judges for either conviction or acquittal; cultural factors determine most of these arrangements. After the Bolshevik revolution the so-called people's assessors were granted a prominent place on all Soviet courts of every level as a check against the professional judiciary. Ther role in the judicial system is now constitutionally guaranteed and in 1965 their total number amounted to about half a million. Like the career judges they are elected from lists proposed by the Party; but the lay assessors usually sit for short terms. According to reports their role has become rather passive, but official writings stress their importance as partners of a career judiciary which is selected more and more on the basis of professional qualifications. Although the assessors are usually a cut above ordinary factory workers, they seem to be frequently overawed by the judges' professional expertise.[47]

In general little is known about the influence which laymen are able to exercise on the mixed benches of various countries. In Sweden the lay judges are reported to agree almost invariably with the presiding magistrate;[48] this also may be explained by the fact that the career judiciary is in tune with community sentiments. The attitudes of the French judiciary toward lay members on the bench are similar to those which they had

[47] Hazard, 1960, pp. 35ff.
[48] Schmidt and Strömholm, 1964, pp. 9–10.

assumed toward the jury: they consider them too emotional, too easily swayed by the histrionics of an adroit attorney, and hence in need of strong guidance.[49] But judges in West Germany, where laymen also serve on certain appellate courts, have on the whole a more favorable opinion of the contribution which the assessors are able to make.[50]

In Vermont, the only state in the United States where mixed tribunals function, the knowledge of the elected "Assistant Judges" is considered useful to determine local customs. The projected overhauling of the Canadian judicial system might include a more general use of the mixed bench for various kinds of court proceedings.

In all cases where the regular court system opens the bench to lay participation it is the undifferentiated citizen-voter who is selected for court duty. But where specialized tribunals such as labor courts, commercial courts, and various administrative courts recruit lay assessors because of their competence for judging the cases that come before these tribunals, the judicial system becomes a vehicle of functional representation. Because of an acknowledged need for this kind of representation and because of its potential for creating meaningful participation, it can be expected that the use of mixed benches with specially qualified lay assessors will become fairly widespread in many legal systems. (For some further discussion of this form of adjudication, see below, Chapter 6.)

By contrast the method of entrusting the settlement of conflicts of small importance and the sanction of minor offenses to the sole judgment of unpaid lay judges is on the decline, at least in the Western world. The French Fifth Republic did away with the *justices de paix* because of their generally unsatisfactory performance. Similar reforms in other countries are in line with a general trend of replacing the amateur by the professional. In England and the United States where the number of professional judges has not kept pace with the needs, the institution of lay justices has prevented the clogging of the judicial machinery and is not about to disappear completely.[51] It has often been attacked—"the place for the lay mind is emphatically in the jury and not on the bench," a socialist critic concluded several decades ago.[52] Reforms aiming at a more careful and less politically motivated selection of the lay magistrates in England and in the United States have been proposed and sometimes carried through. Where urban magistrate courts have not been professionalized, or turned into mixed special-function benches, provision for some training of the lay judges has

---

[49] See Casamayor, 1970, p. 43.

[50] Casper and Zeisel, 1972, pp. 138f., and more critically p. 184.

[51] On the situation in England, see Jackson, 1967, pp. 178ff.

[52] Laski, 1932, p. 465.

been made. Their contribution to conflict settlement is most satisfactory, however, in those rural areas where their ties with local government authorities have remained close.

Only in socialist countries has the scope of what might be called communal justice increased. During Khrushchev's rule, Comrades' Courts were set up all through the Soviet Union—in factories, on collective farms, in housing collectives, etc.—to deal with a great number of minor disturbances of the public order, including family discords. By 1965 more than 200,000 of these "revivalist-type tribunals" were reported to be in existence,[53] all of them manned by elected representatives of the communities for which they act. Their resolutions, passed by majority vote, result in minor punishments, fines, or reprimands that cannot be appealed. While they undoubtedly trespass on the province of the regular courts, Soviet officials have generally praised them because they can deal with a great number of conflict situations without being bound by the standards of due process which the regular courts are now pledged to observe. The career judiciary has at times been critical of them. But so far the success of these courts is attested to by the progressive enlargement of their prerogatives in the Soviet Union. In countries of Eastern Europe with a stronger civil-law tradition, the introduction of similar tribunals has been greeted with greater reserve.

The Maoist regime has gone farthest in "taking the courts to the people." [54] Mass public trials during which the peasants in the fields chant their verdict of guilty are not entirely unlike those conducted by the large juries of classical Greece which Plato and Aristotle described as an ancient institution of lay justice.

---

[53] See the interesting discussion of the comradely courts by Conquest, 1968, pp. 118ff.

[54] Hazard, 1969, pp. 138ff.

THE WAYS AND MEANS OF THE LAW II

6

	Any judicial decision is designed to individualize a
THE MAKING	general norm for the purpose of settling concrete
OF A JUDICIAL	controversies, each of them unique in some sense.
DECISION	Thousands of such decisions, which make up the

THE MAKING OF A JUDICIAL DECISION

Any judicial decision is designed to individualize a general norm for the purpose of settling concrete controversies, each of them unique in some sense. Thousands of such decisions, which make up the bulk of the law in all systems, appear, and often are, truly routine: the facts underlying a conflict between plaintiff and defendant or a situation which gives rise to criminal prosecution are undisputed; there is little doubt as to which rules apply to the situation. Moreover a fairly large proportion of the business with which judicial institutions in many countries are concerned does not really involve disputes but rather amounts to routine administration. In the American context uncontested divorces, wage attachments, evictions, default judgments, bankruptcies and many criminal misdemeanors are examples.[1] In such cases the process of decision-making by a court has the characteristics of a quasi-automatic act. It has been compared to the workings of a slot machine into which the facts of the case are fed and which produces, painlessly as it were, the appropriate decision.

Controversies about the true nature of the judicial process are usually concerned with that relatively small but critical mass of situations where the outcome of a true controversy is uncertain and where no automatic solution should be expected. Here either the facts of the case or the norms to be applied, and quite frequently both facts and norms, are in dispute. In such cases the situation which the judge has to face is in a great number of legal cultures strikingly similar. Astonishingly enough the way in which an American philosopher-judge has formulated the questions to be settled ap-

---

[1] Abel, 1974, p. 228.

pears to have almost universal application: "What is it that I do when I decide a case?" Benjamin Cardozo asked in 1921.

> *To what sources of information do I appeal for guidance? To what proportion do I permit them to contribute to the result? In what proportion ought they to contribute? If a precedent is applicable, when do I refuse to follow it? If no precedent is applicable, how do I reach the rule that will make a precedent for the future? If I am seeking logical consistency, the symmetry of the legal structure, how far shall I seek it? At what point shall the quest be halted by some discrepant custom, by some consideration of the social welfare, by my own or the common standards of justice and morals?* [2]

Although the questions that Justice Cardozo raised have general validity, the answers given to them vary greatly in different cultures and at different periods. One court's priorities will be different from those of another, and often the same judge might look at them differently from one decision to the next. The variables determining the choices are numerous indeed. To admit that such choices exist and that they make up, as Cardozo put it, the "strange compound which is brewed daily in the caldron of the courts," assumes that judges are, by their decisions, creating law. They are not merely the "mouthpiece" of law created elsewhere, which is the role Montesquieu wanted to restrict them to when he described judges as being "deprived of power." [3] Sir William Blackstone, though speaking for another legal culture (England in the late eighteenth century), did not think otherwise: in his view judges were the oracles of the law, "not delegated to pronounce a new law, but to maintain and expound the old one."

The Federalist Papers adhered to a similar view even while granting the courts the power of judicial review. And as willful and deliberate a judge as Chief Justice Marshall insisted: "Courts are the mere instruments of law and can will nothing." One merely needs to realize how drastically some of Marshall's decisions affected his country's destiny to recognize that he underplayed intentionally the role of the judiciary. His own interests and those of the men closest to him in the power structure of the young republic were well served by the fiction that the judiciary was devoid of "will."

Today it is widely admitted that the line between a mere application or individualization of preexisting norms and the creation of norms cannot be drawn and that to conclude otherwise ignores the realities of politics *and* legal life in any system. The notion that judges are mere "operators of the law" and that there is only one solution of any legal dispute has been

---

[2] Cardozo (1921), 1971, p. 10.

[3] Montesquieu (1753), 1949, Book VI, Ch. 6.

termed correctly to be little more than an "accepted folklore." [4] But like any folklore it still has an important effect on the way people—and in this case, judges—act, even though it does not accurately describe their actions. How influential the folklore remains depends primarily on the role of the judiciary in a given political system and on the value system which role assumptions have produced over time. On this subject a statement explaining the behavior of American appellate judges has rather general validity:

> *The place to begin is with the fact that the men of our appellate bench are human beings. I have never understood why the cynics talk and think as if this were not so. For it is so. And one of the more obvious and obstinate facts about human beings is that they operate in and respond to traditions, and especially to such traditions as are offered to them by the crafts . . . they follow.*[5]

The differing traditions of the judicial craft and especially the methods of recruiting and advancing judges in civil-law and in common-law countries (discussed above, Chapter 4) explain in large part why in the former a belief in the mechanical quality of judicial decision-making has survived somewhat more stubbornly. The conventional mentality of a civil servant, long prevalent among continental judges, will wish to do little more than preserve at least the outward appearances of being a faithful "mouthpiece." By contrast in a common-law system where the case and the judge are central in the legal life of society, where "the judge is hero, and the opinion is his weapon," the judge is encouraged and stimulated to leave his mark on the law in a way in which his continental colleagues are not.[6] But because of the greater insight into the actual role of the judge (provided by the studies of social scientists), such differences as may have existed have come under critical scrutiny. Observers of the judicial system of postwar Italy have concluded that there is little left of the traditional "folklore" and that Italian judges know quite well what they are doing.[7] A one-time judge of the German Constitutional Court has spoken of the survival of former beliefs as the "Number 1 Lebenslüge," a rank hypocrisy, indulged in by too many of his colleagues. On the other hand a long-time student of comparative law has commented on the existence of a similar self-delusion on the part of many American and English judges when he attributed to the common law a "special aptness to hide behind a screen of verbal formulae of

[4] Merryman, 1969, p. 86.

[5] Karl Llewellyn, quoted from Fellman, 1968, p. 48.

[6] von Mehren, 1957, p. 43.

[7] Cappelletti, Merryman, and Perillo, 1967, p. 249.

apparent logically *formal* rationality, those considerations of *substantive* rationality, that is, of social policy, by which the decision has been actually motivated but which judges are reluctant to reveal to the public and, often enough to themselves." [8]

It is very likely that such a reluctance to admit what one is doing in fact is caused in part by an adherence to the doctrine of the separation of powers which is honored as a principle not only in the West but also in socialist countries. It produces on the part of the judges in many parts of the world an "instinctive as well as trained reluctance" [9] to acknowledge how often they must cross the line between norm adjudication and *de facto* law-making when the case before them cannot be subsumed easily under an existing rule.

When one wishes to look behind rationalizations and to examine the actual amount of judicial discretion, one finds that cultural traditions of the craft are important factors to be considered. In addition the demands of the historical moment, the particularities of the case to be decided, the place of the court in the judicial hierarchy, and not least the personality of the "human being" deciding the case—all these will have an impact in determining where the decision can be placed on a continuum that stretches from strict positivism to free-wheeling creativity.

It is now generally recognized that one must not overemphasize the importance which legal techniques and ways of reasoning have for the outcome. At one time it was maintained that decisive differences in judicial decision-making arose from the fact that the common-law way of arguing from precedent was predominantly inductive, while the civil-law judge who was bound to apply codes and statutes was tied to a deductive method. To attempt such a distinction overlooks first of all the fact (discussed above, Chapter 2) that today in common-law countries also the most important controversies which are brought to court have to be decided on the basis of statutory enactments, administrative regulations, and the like. On the other hand, as we shall see below, judges in civil-law countries frequently must pay attention to previously decided cases.

Some intellectual tools have proven useful to judges throughout the ages and in many different cultures. Reasoning by analogy and employing fictions are fairly generalized forms of judicial reasoning. By the former it is possible to create new legal categories which, if functional, can acquire a life of their own to regulate new situations: responsibility for the "behavior" of one's automobile might be likened to responsibility for the behavior of one's domestic animals. Fictions have furthered legal change especially in less developed systems where neither a legislature nor a stream of re-

---

[8] Max Rheinstein in Weber (1922), 1954, p. lvi (emphasis supplied).

[9] Felix Frankfurter, quoted here from Friedmann, 1967, p. 461.

ported court cases are available: [10] in the absence of provisions for disposing of property outside of the nuclear family after death, the intended heir might be considered as an "adopted" son. By and large such techniques are not culture-bound. They make it possible to cling to old forms while in fact innovating, and to satisfy at the same time the need for stability, utility, and possibly equity.

The triad of values which has been described (see above, Chapter 3) as being the aspiration of all law, also finds, or at any rate ought to find, an expression in judicial decisions. In most systems and situations, the judge, especially when compared with the legislator or even certain administrators, will be found on the side of stability rather than on the side of innovative distributive justice. For as one of the most reform-minded of our present-day Supreme Court Justices has remarked, judges "share the yearning for security that is common to all people everywhere. And this yearning grows as the world seems to grow more insecure." [11] This is not just a question of temperament, however, but is inherent in the setting of the judicial process and in the means available to it. One of Justice Douglas's equally vigorous predecessors, Oliver W. Holmes, had once defined the very essence of law as being the "prophesies of what the courts will do in fact." But later, towards the end of his long career, he added: "I recognize without hesitation that judges do and must legislate, but they can do so only interstitially; they are confined from molar to molecular motions." [12]

The hierarchical organization of court systems, an almost worldwide phenomenon, limits the freedom of most judges to become knight-errants roaming at will through the realm of norms to bring about results that appear desirable to them. If at all possible judges wish to avoid being overruled. Where concern for promotion is a fact of judicial life, one will find an understandable reluctance to stand out as a nonconformist. This restraint may also be born out of respect for the mastery of the higher-placed members of the craft, or it may simply be due to a dislike of seeing one's efforts wasted.

Such concerns explain why even in systems where judicial precedents are not formally binding, those set by higher courts have a definite impact on judicial decision-making. They are cited in briefs and decisions and studied by all those concerned, including the students of law. In the Soviet Union courts are not permitted to cite previous decisions, because to do so might give the appearance that the judiciary and not just the people as represented by the Soviets are setting the law. But it appears doubtful

[10] See Cohen, 1931, pp. 227f, a particularly enlightening article on a legal institution by a philosopher.

[11] Douglas, 1949, pp. 735ff.

[12] Quoted here from Fellman, 1968, p. 45.

whether in reality this makes a difference, since hierarchical thinking is strongly enough developed even without citing court records.

Some Latin American systems experiment with a special form of judicial consensus-building: they may state that a decision has no effect beyond the specific dispute it has settled; but when the highest court has given a certain interpretation of the law a given number of times it becomes a binding precedent. And nothing prevents a forceful opinion by the higher court from exercising its influence before the given number of times. An alternative to voluntary or enforced conformity always remains open, at least in democratic regimes. The judge who wishes to engage in creative innovation may attempt to make his decision sufficiently persuasive to win approval of the higher court.

All judges, including those sitting on the highest courts of their country, reach their decisions by following what some of them do not hesitate to call their hunches. But a commitment to their craft and to their own effectiveness compels them to convert such hunches into a reasoned and, hopefully, persuasive position. Beyond deciding the case that has come before them, many judges also wish to make a contribution to the development of a legal doctrine and of law itself. For thereby they extend, for good or evil, their ruling into the future, knowing that without it even the settlement which they have just achieved will remain precarious and might be disturbed anew.

It has been noted that the standard of "reasonableness" for judging the behavior of the parties appearing in court, and also for evaluating the meaning of precedents or the language of statutes, has found its way into many otherwise disparate legal orders.[13] "Reasonableness" may be as vague as "due process," yet it permits an enunciation of principles upon which a judicial decision tries to align itself.

The scope of judicial interpretation varies not only with cultural traditions but also with the temper of the time. Byzantine culture at its height, enlightened absolutism in eighteenth-century Europe, the French Jacobins, and Napoleon were all equally reluctant to entrust judges with interpreting unclear legal provisions. If the need arose judges should elicit authoritative advice from the political organs of government (see also above, Chapter 2). An article of Napoleon's Civil Code went farther yet when it warned the judges specifically (art. 5) that it was "forbidden to lay down general rules of conduct while deciding the concrete cases submitted to them." A century later another code country, Switzerland, developed in its opening article an opposite model for the judicial process:

The Code governs all questions of law which come within the letter or the spirit of any of its provisions. —If the Code does not furnish an applicable

---

[13] E.g., compare Gluckman, 1955 (describing tribal legal procedure in Africa), with Cardozo (1921), 1971.

provision, the judge shall decide in accordance with customary law, and failing that, according to the rule which he would establish as a legislator. [*Emphasis supplied*]

The yet more recent Italian Code contains a similar provision.

During the first part of the nineteenth century a conservative French judiciary was quite content to hew close to the sober wording of the codes. In doing so it wanted to give to the state seeming permanence and rigidity. Their way of handling cases was also well suited to the slow development of the French economy. But when, under the Second Empire, rapid industrialization and a more dynamic development set in, judicial inventiveness gave new content to old provisions. In their endeavors the judges were assisted by legal scholars who discovered a sociological dimension to the law and reached conclusions not unlike those elaborated later by the realist school in the United States. In every legal system the development of tort law offers a good example of legal modernization because it deals with problems very close to the daily life of a society. Five brief articles in the French *Code Civil* had regulated this field in a way which was inappropriate to the needs of an expanding industrial society. To obtain damages of any kind it was necessary to prove that the defendant had been guilty at the very least of grossly negligent behavior. The wording of the law denied any claim to the victims of accidents, industrial and otherwise, in an environment which was creating ever-greater risks. But like a common-law judiciary the French courts modified by a long line of cases, and sometimes by trial and error, the original code provisions, acting thereby in effect as "legislators," until the results were in line with the needs of modern technology.

Certain broadly worded articles strewn throughout the German Civil Code, enacted in the midst of vigorous economic expansion at home and imperialist ventures abroad, specifically encouraged judicial creativity. Clauses requiring "good faith" in the fulfillment of contractual obligations and recommendations that "ordinary usage" (something like reasonableness) be the yardstick for evaluating behavior and that no juristic acts be upheld that violated *bonas mores* (respectable behavior) amounted to little else than a legislative delegation of policy-making to the courts. Each of these general clauses encouraged the building of an impressive body of case law which set widely commented on and emulated, if not formally binding, precedents. When after the First World War runaway inflation shook the very foundations of the German economic order, the judiciary found ways to bring order out of chaos without waiting for legislative remedies merely by applying the broad language of the good faith clause of the code, then a quarter of a century old. German statutes, such as the Law against Unfair Competition, gave the judiciary similarly extensive powers of creating new law: while the statute prescribed the consequences of behavior to be classified as unfair competition, it left to the courts the definition of what was to be regarded as objectionable. There is here a striking parallel to the American antitrust legislation as developed by the courts. By contrast, judges in prewar Japan, a country which had adopted an almost literal translation of the German Civil Code, voluntarily limited their discretion in deciding cases since they considered themselves servants of the state, not guardians of justice.[14] Other civil-law courts have developed a number of concepts in similarly piecemeal fashion. By modifying contractual obligations they were able to correct economic iniquities and dislocations. They also have sometimes been more willing than American judges to disregard statutory rules which have become obsolete and whose application would have led to patently unjust consequences because of drastically changed conditions.

A comparison with judicial behavior prevalent in common-law countries reveals some differences; yet they are neither quite as striking nor as uniform as is often assumed. It has been explained earlier (see above, Chapter 2) why English judges had come to regard the development of law by precedent to be best suited to their own interests, both as individuals and as members of their craft. Small in number and remarkably homogeneous, the English judiciary was proud of its reputation for consistency and predictability. They viewed faithfulness to principles, once established, as a wholesome restraint on arbitrariness; they distrusted judicial creativity. Well into our century English judges were inclined to let a precedent stand even if the ensuing rigidity made it difficult to apply norms developed in times of patriarchical households. Their generally sceptical outlook on the benefits of legislation, the reasons for which have also been discussed, made English judges almost unseemingly cautious about statutory interpretation. They shied away from delving into the legislative history of complicated statutes and instead gave to the text a literal meaning, even when this frustrated the patent purpose of the law. Once established, such construction was likely to be regarded as another binding precedent. The narrowness of many rulings by English courts is undoubtedly one of the reasons why at least the ordinary courts handle less litigation than courts in other countries of similar development.

Nonetheless, and especially in more recent times, a highly qualified judiciary has not entirely denied itself the possibility of finding appropriate solutions to modern problems. In order to avoid undesirable results several ways were open to English judges, just as they are to all judges who wish to combine the appearance of consistency with an urge for innovation. They either demonstrated that the case before them could and should be distinguished from the precedent from which they wished to depart. Or they

14 Danielski, 1969, p. 48.

narrowed the core of the previous decision, the *ratio decidendi,* so much that it no longer presented an obstacle to change. Hence the pretense that the law was a seamless web of precedents tied to each other was in reality quite frequently a fiction. The English judge was hampered not so much by an absence of freedom but rather by the "haphazard, sporadic and, sometimes, tortuous way in which he must work"[15] so as not to violate certain taboos set by his profession. In order to release the House of Lords, the highest British Court, from the obligation to be bound by its own decisions, the Lord Chancellor declared in 1966:

> *Their Lordships . . . recognize that too rigid adherence to precedent may lead to injustice in a particular case and also unduly restrict the proper development of the law. They propose therefore to modify their present practice and, while treating former decisions of this House as normally binding, to depart from a previous decision when it appears right to do so.*[16]

So far the pronouncement appears not to have had a wide-ranging influence. Long-established traditions concerning appropriate ways of finding and developing law are not easily altered.

It is perhaps not surprising that in countries of the British Commonwealth the fate of the law in the courts has been somewhat different. While these countries belong to the common-law family, the judiciary even when trained in England come from a more varied background and the societies with which they interact are less homogeneous. As long as judicial disputes could, as a last resort, be referred to the Privy Council in London, the more mechanistic interpretation of the common law and the strict adherence to precedent had to be honored to a certain degree. But years before such an appeal to London was eliminated, a younger group of Canadian jurists had successfully insisted on a more flexible interpretation of both the common law and statutory law. Their efforts were inspired not only by the less reverential attitude towards precedent in the province of Quebec, but also by a similar example given south of the Canadian border, in the United States. When India won independence an entire generation of lawyers and judges had been brought up in the conservative English tradition quite foreign to indigenous law. As has been mentioned earlier (see Chapter 1), the national law of present-day India has in all essentials remained within the common-law family. The Indian constitution specifically preaches the adherence to precedent when it provides (art. 141) that "the law declared by the Supreme Court is binding on all courts in India." Yet in reality Indian

---

[15] Friedmann, 1967, p. 464.

[16] Ibid.

judges, and especially the younger ones, are eager to help in legitimizing reforms by giving a broad interpretation to modern welfare legislation and by ignoring precedents when they stand in their way.[17]

In the United States the concern for strict adherence to precedent has always been less developed and judicial creativity correspondingly greater than in the motherland of the common law. A federally organized country of continental dimensions, one composed of economically and socially dissimilar regions, lent itself badly to a common alignment on previous decisions which were often unknown from one state to another. The recruitment of strong and frequently politically minded personalities into the judiciary promoted judicial activism even among conservative worshippers of the common law.[18] Judicial review unknown in England sharpened an awareness of the political, sociological, and philosophical components in the law. The ensuing duty incumbent upon American courts to decide vital problems of public policy, which in England will ordinarily be settled by the political branches of government, has encouraged a certain type of judicial partisanship at the expense of judicial formalism. (For a further discussion of judicial review see below, Chapter 7.) Comparing the two countries' attitudes towards precedent and interpretation before an audience of British jurists, the Chief Justice of an American State Supreme Court was probably correct when he stated that in this respect American judicial attitudes were probably closer to continental than to English practices. But, as we have seen earlier, the existing differences are sometimes altogether exaggerated.

It must be realized, moreover, that generalizations about the judiciary of a nation, let alone of all the systems belonging to the same legal family, do not come close to the realities and varieties of judicial decision-making. Some studies have attempted to establish a link between the role perceptions of American state supreme court judges, their activities on the court, and the political cultures of the states, as revealed by the judges' attitudes towards the scope of government activity. On the basis of in-depth interviews respondent judges were classified as law interpreters (adhering generally to an attitude of judicial self-restraint), law makers (i.e., judicial activists), and "pragmatists," the latter being a residual category of the first two.[19] It appears likely that similar role perceptions could be found and corresponding classification could be attempted in many legal systems and

---

[17] See Gadbois, 1970, pp. 149ff.

[18] See Jaffe, 1969, p. 67.

[19] See Vines, 1969, p. 471, and the discussion of his findings by Grossman and Sarat, 1971, pp. 195f. and 200. In Germany some similar highly interesting but at least as yet not easily comparable studies are underway; see Riegel, Werle, and Wildenmann, 1974, especially. Tables H1–H9. For a report on the methods and assumptions of this inquiry, see Wildenmann, 1973.

subsystems. In the American studies no relationship was found between the role assumptions and either party affiliation or the method of selection. Which variables of the political and legal cultures are among the determinants either of judicial urge for innovation or of cautiousness, remains an important topic for comparative study. However, while causal analysis is generally difficult in all social-science research, this is particularly true when one seeks to identify what has "caused" a particular judicial decision. At present we still lack the most basic data for comparison.

Generalities that judges ought to be sensitive to the "great tides and currents which engulf the rest of men" and that a judge must "manifest the half-framed purposes of his time" are true enough; [20] but even when they come, as those do, from gifted practitioners, they do not tell us enough about the merits and possible demerits of judicial flexibility in a given historical situation and a particular society. At least in a democracy it might be generally true that discretion will be greatest where the "general principles of jurisprudence are unclear, constitutional, statutory or administrative phrases vague, precedents unimpressive and history uncertain." [21] A respected American Appellate Court judge for whom judicial discretion was tantamount to desirable creativity has expressed his admiration for what he understood as the guiding principles of traditional Chinese law, to wit, that all "legal principles should be treated as mere general guides, to be applied suitably and with special attention to the unique facts of a case." [22]

In a society in which a consensus on basic values has remained strong, it might be possible, and under certain circumstances advisable, to accord the judiciary a large amount of leeway. Judges may be counted upon to know that even though most of them cannot be voted out of office, they should never exercise their discretion in a way that too drastically opposed popular feelings as confided to the ballot box.[23] But in countries that are beset by divisive conflicts, a freewheeling judiciary might, under the guise of independence, become the handmaiden of revolution or counterrevolution.

During the republican regime installed in Germany after the First World War, a generally arch-conservative judiciary played a role destructive of the political order. A method of "freelaw finding" had been promoted during the first decades of the century by liberal German jurists seeking to drive formalism out of the courtrooms. After the war judges hostile to the

---

[20] Cardozo (1921), 1971, p. 168, and, in similar terms, various British and American judges quoted in Mendelson, 1968, p. 321.

[21] Murphy, 1968, p. 316.

[22] See Frank, 1956, p. 915.

[23] For a modern statement of the need for judicial self-restraint in a democracy, see Justice Frankfurter dissenting in the so-called Flag Salute case: 319 U.S. 624, 646–71 (1943).

new political order used their discretion with the purpose of falsifying wherever possible the intentions of republican reform legislation. In criminal cases broadly framed statutes enabled them to give free rein to their political bias. By rewarding the enemies of the republic instead of protecting its supporters the judiciary contributed to the early fall of the republic and the triumph of Hitler.[24]

On the surface the views which totalitarian and authoritarian regimes are taking towards the judicial process appear contradictory. Any highly centralized system can only distrust the delegated form of decision-making with which the judiciary is necessarily entrusted. Unlike the French revolutionaries of the eighteenth century, modern authoritarian rulers know that it would be impracticable to compel judges to turn for the interpretation of norms to the political organs of government or to the party. Instead the judges are relied upon to give to law and to facts that interpretation which suits best the values and policies upheld by the regime.

After his rise to power Hitler assured those German judges who had not been purged during the first months of his rule that they would continue to enjoy the privilege of immovability from office. Yet he added that in applying the law they should show utmost "elasticity." Soon thereafter the "will of the Führer" was declared to be a positive source of law which the judiciary had to translate into concrete decisions. The "sound feelings of the people" were prescribed as a standard of judgment in all matters, even the most trivial, that came before the courts.

As we have seen earlier, there have been periods when judges in the Soviet Union were similarly compelled to serve slavishly the political ends of society. Among various techniques used judges resorted to the punishment of offenders for behavior that was classified as "analogous" to crimes defined in codes and statutes. At other times, and especially more recently, judges have been admonished to employ discretion more sparingly and always in a way that does not interfere with desirable stability and predictability. In order to give the judges proper guidance many of the presently valid statutes are prefaced by a lengthy preamble which explains the intentions of the legislator. Of even more immediate significance are the explicit directives which the Supreme Court of the Soviet Union issues from time to time as a commentary on desirable principles for adjudication. Altogether it appears still to be true that judges, whatever their formal independence, can be relied upon to be inspired in their decisions by the interests of the Soviet society, as reflected in party policy. When such goals became temporarily blurred, as during the last months of Khrushchev's rule, at least certain Soviet judges were able to assert themselves by giving a voluntarily narrow construction to the so-called antiparasite law which they seem to

---

[24] See the remarkable and foresighted article by Fraenkel (1927), 1968, pp. 1–41.

have abhorred because of its ominous vagueness which permitted the prosecution of non-conformists.[25]

STYLE OF DECISION MAKING

To render judicial decisions in writing is characteristic of all modern law. To append an explanation of the reasons on which the decision is grounded is a widespread practice. This is why one of the outstanding exceptions to that rule, the verdict of the Anglo-American jury, has been likened to a decision by oracle (see above, Chapter 5). Another common feature of many courts, at least of those on the appellate level, is their collegial makeup. In lower-level courts the role of the judge may still be close enough to that of a mediator or a fatherly figure so that the decision can be entrusted to his unassisted judgment. But when the appreciation of the facts and the finding of the correct norms assume greater importance, where the interests involved are weightier, the offense more serious, and generally on the appellate level, most systems seek insurance against the possibilities of human error by calling upon a group of judges, either professional or lay.

It can safely be assumed that on all collegial courts there will be disagreements as to the desirable outcome, whether such disagreements occur only occasionally or frequently and whether they pertain to the appreciation of the facts, to the applicable norms, or to both. If such controversies can be considered as a natural outcome of all judicial disputes, nevertheless quite important and revealing differences exist in regard to the problem of how the existing controversies should be dealt with. The solution depends to a large extent on a number of largely culture-bound choices.[26] Is the communication of several possibly contradictory opinions likely to strengthen or to weaken the acceptance of the judgment as legitimate? How will the public expression of minority opinions or their suppression in favor of one agreed-upon version affect intracourt relations? Does society derive enough value from being able to recognize possibly unpopular dissent, and from being able to understand the nature of the law as a human institution open to doubt, to outweigh all possible objections to the publication of several opinions?

On the basis of sociological as well as psychological findings the students of small groups have argued quite convincingly that members of such a group exhibit a tendency to reach agreement or consensus. Since collegiate courts have many of the characteristics of small groups, generalizations that

[25] Barry and Berman, 1971, pp. 325ff.

[26] See, also for what follows, Kirchheimer, 1961, p. 428. For a good comparative discussion of the problem of judicial dissent, see also Nadelmann, 1959, pp. 415ff.

have been reached about the latter can also apply to the behavior of judges. Hence the assumption that collegiate courts everywhere tend strongly towards unanimity seems entirely justified.[27] Where unanimity prevails it obviates the need for deciding what to do about dissent. But where this is not the case the common-law systems permit the public voicing of judicial controversies; all other systems, with a few exceptions, frown upon it.

Studies have shown some variations in the frequency of dissent among state appellate courts in the United States. High rates of dissent have been reported from states with great socioeconomic diversity and with high levels of partisanship and political competition. But the explanations that have been offered are only partially satisfactory.[28] Such variations as exist certainly suggest that the reasons for them have to be sought in part outside of the courts themselves. The nature of the problems to be decided and the historical circumstances under which they arise will make a difference even for the same state or the same court.

This also holds true for the U.S. Supreme Court. The frequency of dissent or unanimity has never been independent of the personality of the judges on the court and has sometimes been influenced by the outlook, the style, and the forcefulness of the Chief Justice. But primarily accord or discord have reflected the temper of the times. It is well known what role the "great dissents" of such judges as Holmes and Brandeis have played in constitutional developments. During recent decades unanimous decisions have been rendered in only a minority of so-called full-opinion cases. One of the most frequent dissenters of our times, Justice Douglas, called the right to dissent "the only thing that makes life tolerable for a judge of an appellate court." To him "dissents or concurring opinions may salvage for tomorrow the principle that was sacrificed or forgotten today." Chief Justice Hughes, who during his periods on the Court rarely dissented himself, also described dissent in a court of last resort as "an appeal to the brooding spirit of the law, to the intelligence of a future day, when a later decision may possibly correct the error into which the dissenting judge believes the court to have been betrayed." [29]

Dissenting opinions are frequently biting and sarcastic, and the same may occasionally be true for a concurrring opinion, in which a judge tells his brethren that although he happened to reach the same result as they did, he feels constrained to point out how little esteem he has for their

---

[27] See Ulmer, 1971, pp. 12ff.

[28] For references to partly unpublished materials and their discussion, see Grossman and Sarat, 1971, p. 192.

[29] For these and other quotations of statements by prominent American jurists about the value of dissents, see Abraham, 1968, p. 204, and Nadelman, 1959, p. 431.

reasoning. There is no doubt that such methods have occasionally lowered the Court's prestige and that its role as an educator of the public mind is possibly slighted. Yet this price is paid in order to give full expression to the existence of plural values in the legal life of a democratic community.

In view of what has been said earlier about the makeup of the English judiciary it is not astonishing that while the publication of dissenting and concurring opinions is allowed, it is a far less frequent occurrence. Moreover, before 1960 decisions by the Privy Council, which for a time played a fairly significant role in preserving the unity of the common law in the Common-wealth countries, did not provide for the expression of minority opinions. The practice in countries like India, Ireland, and Canada is bewilderingly different and deserves further study before conclusions about any cultural conditioning can be drawn. In spite of the divisiveness of Indian politics more than 90 percent of reported court decisions by federal courts there have been unanimous. In Ireland the publication of dissenting opinions was discontinued after independence. By contrast the Canadian Supreme Court is little given to seeking agreement; the Chief Justice neither suggests nor obtains cooperation or consultation by his colleagues, and the opinion reached by a majority of judges is not singled out as the official opinion. Sometimes the Court's devotion to pluralism has been qualified as a form of "judicial anarchy"—which is undoubtedly an exaggeration.

The only country in continental Europe, East and West, which permits the voicing of different judicial opinions in deciding a case is Switzerland. The Federal Appeals Court and some of the cantonal (state) courts delib-erate and vote in public on all decisions, a practice also known in early Roman and early Germanic times. Hence those present in the courtroom, and this means at least the parties, are able to witness judicial controversies and their outcome, even though only the majority opinion will be published. It is not accidental that the only continental country which does not follow the civil-servant career pattern for the selection of its judges, also has a different outlook on the style of decision-making.

For the traditional European concept of the judicial process the very idea of admitting publicly that a given case could have been decided in more than one way runs counter to the principles of rationality, anonymity, and secrecy. Upon their appointment judges are usually compelled to swear not to reveal any differences of opinion between the members of a collegiate court. When at the end of the last century the drafters of a new German Code of Civil Procedure were discussing a proposal to adhere to the com-mon-law pattern of publishing dissents, the suggestion was rejected unanim-ously and in terms that highlight the contrast between the outlook of the European and of the American judges quoted above; the proposal, it was said,

was incompatible with the authority of the courts and good relations be-
tween judges; [it] would lead to Byzantinism and to the seeking of publicity.
It would foster vanity and disputatiousness. As few decisions would be
unanimous, dissenting opinions would become the rule. . . . The court
faces the outside world as a single authority, whose decisions are the deci-
sions of the court. A court's principal function is to decide the individual
case justly and to uphold the authority of the laws, not to provoke sci-
entific discussions over legal questions.[30]

Such concerns mirror, among other things, the mentality of a judiciary
which shares the beliefs and attitudes of a career bureaucracy. In present-
day France some judges of liberal outlook express the opinion that judicial
independence would be in jeopardy if published minority opinions were to
expose their authors to a variety of pressures from within and without the
judiciary.

It is true that the assumption of the monolithic nature of law is defeated also in Europe each time that an appellate court reverses the decision
of a lower court; this is so because this is an admission that conflict settlement other than the one originally proposed is not only possible but correct.
In order to maintain the fiction of an unerring and majestic law some high
courts, among them the French *Cour de Cassation,* do not actually replace
the decision which they have found erroneous but indicate to the lower
court why it ought to reverse itself and how it should rewrite its judgment.
This corresponds to the intellectually cruel but widely reported habit of
many European collegiate courts to assign the writing of the court's opinion
to judges who during the deliberations had expressed their doubts or disagreements with the majority.

However, during recent decades a slow change in attitudes seems to
have taken place. United States occupation authorities had imposed on
Japanese courts the "duty" to publish dissenting opinions. The practice was
very slow in developing, but after initial hesitations were overcome, it is
now fairly widespread. Opinion polls in Western Germany reveal that a
majority of judges still reject the idea of publishing dissenting and concurring opinions as wasteful, if not dangerous. But the number of those who
think otherwise is growing, especially among younger jurists and among
associate justices who sometimes seem to resent the "yoke" of their presiding judges.[31] When the law instituting the new West German Constitutional Court was being initiated, a proposal to permit the publication of
dissents was narrowly defeated. But when in 1966 the Court had to decide
controversies arising out of the notorious *Spiegel* affair, the polarization of

[30] Quoted in von Mehren, 1957, p. 834.

[31] See Weyrauch, 1964, pp. 217–23, and Werle, 1973, pp. 13–14.

views was so great that the court published the two decisions on which it had split evenly (with the presiding judge obligated to break the tie). There has been pressure to make the publication of dissents a regular procedure of the Constitutional Court at least under certain special conditions. A new law of 1971 in effect permits the publication of dissenting opinion by the Constitutional Court. But so far very little use has been made of this privilege. Whether the practice would spread to other courts appears doubtful.

There exist still other, frequently connected, differences in the style of judicial decision-making in various legal cultures. Anglo-American decisions are usually long and sometimes discursive. They may engage in a reevaluation of the facts even at the appellate level; a long series of precedents may be cited; and the underlying premises of the judgments and the values of the deciding judges may be discussed fully and, sometimes, frankly. Even when no concurring opinions are published, a single opinion may still lay bare the compromise in which the judges have engaged before reaching their decisions. Such a style usually reveals much about the wide range of judicial law-making that has entered into the decision. It also furnishes precedents which, because of their loose wording, permit the exercise of broad discretion in the future.

By contrast the decisions of civil-law courts, and of those in socialist countries as well, are usually rather brief. This is particularly true of the French and Latin American appellate courts, which may limit their decision to an analysis of applicable code provisions. In West Germany the higher courts are somewhat more explicit when disclosing the basis for their judgment. Civil-law judges will usually rationalize thier unwillingness to engage in lengthy reasoning by pointing to the fact that they are not supposed to create binding precedents, but only to decide the case before them. We have already seen why this is not entirely true. In fact, their brevity and formalistic style is often designed to hide the fear that being too explicit might interfere with discreetness and secretiveness, important ingredients of the expert's power. But if this is so, one can entertain serious doubts as to which style of judicial decision making has the greater claim to rationality.

ALTERNATIVES TO JUDICIAL DECISION MAKING

We started our discussion of the ways and means of the law by pointing out that courts do not have a monopoly on settling legal conflicts (see above, Chapter 5). Whether or not a network of regular courts is available, alternative methods of settlement are sought with increasing frequency, an indication that court proceedings are considered unsatisfactory in many legal systems. The reasons for this might be predominantly practical, but they might also express a more fundamental reluctance to appeal to the courts.

In Western democracies the problems raised by the high costs of almost any law suit have not been truly solved by the multiplication of legal aid facilities. The necessary formality of court proceedings adds to costs and inevitably produces delays that are frequently intolerable. Even the highest professional qualifications of a judge—and there are many judges who do not possess these—do not enable him to decide involved technical questions which in modern times arise even in quite ordinary law suits. The use of outside experts involves additional costs and delays.

Once a case has its "day in court" the judge, for all the discretion at his disposal, will still have to come down on one side or the other most of the time; he will find for the plaintiff or the defendant; his verdict will be guilty or not guilty. Once rendered his opinion will be backed (more or less efficiently) by the complicated machinery of a modern state. But life and its conflicts do not always lend themselves to such a black-white judgment. Hence the settlement provided by the courts might raise as many or more problems than it has tried to solve.

To avoid the multiple dilemma involved in court procedures modern legal systems have recourse primarily to either mediation and arbitration, long practiced the world over, or to adjudication by administrative tribunals, a more modern method which is rapidly becoming ubiquitous.

MEDIATION AND ARBITRATION

While we have previously (Chapter 5) pointed out what distinguishes mediation from arbitration, their common characteristics are at least of equal importance: neither the mediator nor the arbitrator belong to the judiciary or, if they occasionally do, they do not act in their official capacity. Not only the settlement of a particular conflict but whatever legal development might arise out of such a settlement is handled here by representatives of the society rather than by organs of the state. Hence these procedures make operative an insight on which legal sociologists have insisted rightly and which we have quoted at the beginning of our study: the center of gravity of any legal culture and the mainsprings of its development should not be sought in the judicial system installed by the government, but in society itself.[32]

The difference between the judge and the nonofficial "conflict settler" is not just one of status and position. Where the judge must sort out past events and applicable norms so as to decide which rights have been acquired or infringed upon, the mediator/arbitrator will identify the interests at

---

[32] This is the main thesis of the seminal work by Ehrlich (1912), 1936, quoted above in Chapter 1, fn. 3.

stake and make the parties aware of them. This will enable him to evaluate for and with the parties the costs of prolonged conflict and to contrast such costs with the possibilities of finding a solution which promises a safe future not only for the parties but also for society. To put interests rather than norms into the foreground will frequently facilitate compromise. Whereas the independence of a judge seems safeguarded by his keeping at equal distance from both parties and being aloof from their milieu, familiarity with the problems that have resulted in conflict and with the parties themselves is not necessarily a handicap for successful mediation. None of this implies that the mediator/arbitrator will be necessarily gentle and soft. In order to play his role correctly and to induce reluctant parties to settle, he might find it appropriate to use threats and to invoke social sanctions which can be at least as painful as the enforcement of a court order.[33]

If such are the philosophy and the mechanics of out-of-court accommodation, it is understandable why it is highly valued by legal cultures which are reluctant to recognize legal rights of the individual as the basis of social order. (See above, Chapter 3.) Because of the strength of Buddhist and Confucian traditions mediation and arbitration have remained preferred methods of conflict resolution in modernized countries such as Japan and Korea. Their court system is fully developed; the training of judges and lawyers follows a Westernized rationalistic pattern. Yet there is a widespread reluctance to submit legal conflicts to the state courts. It is reported that in Japan private mediation "of one sort or another has been and still is effective in settling the vast majority of disputes." [34] The chosen mediator is usually a man of higher status than the disputants; his effectiveness is enhanced by a remnant of traditional social deference. Hesitations in submitting conflicts to the existing court system are sometimes explained as an atavistic apprehension against troubling the government, the successor to the feudal lord, with the quarrels of its subjects.

More decisive is probably a concern not to endanger the healing of a disturbed social relationship by a hard and fast judicial decision reached by a remote authority. It appears particularly inappropriate to bring controversies arising out of contractual relations before a court. For if the parties once felt close enough to enter into such a relationship, they can be expected to reconcile temporary divergencies, if necessary with appropriate help. It is true that this emphasis on compromise has produced manifold abuses. A special profession, the compromise-makers, has developed and what they practice is often harsh extrajudicial coercion.[35] In Siam high

[33] For an excellent discussion of the philosophy and practice of mediation, see Eckhoff, 1966, pp. 158ff.

[34] Henderson, 1969, p. 449.

[35] On conflict settlement in Japan in general, see Kawashima, 1964, pp. 41ff.; for Korea see Hahm, 1969, pp. 36ff.

Bangkok judges find ways of upholding Buddhist traditions behind a facade of orderly court procedure even while ostentatiously applying codified law. Disputants appearing before them are urged to settle their differences among themselves in approved Thai manner which means taking into consideration all the existential circumstances, past, present, and future. Once they have reached such an agreement the court will simply endorse it.[36]

In contemporary India, and especially in rural areas, nonofficial arbitration has survived and outranks in importance settlement by the modern court system. Quite frequently traditional bodies, such as the transformed caste associations, assume the role of an effective arbitrator. There is a widespread feeling that since parties to a dispute will have to live side by side in their communities, all conflict resolution must be ambiguous enough to provide some satisfaction to both sides.[37] The fact that in many of the new African states mediation and arbitration by village elders play a similarly prominent role suggests that such methods are not necessarily tied to specific religious traditions but may correspond to the needs or to the authority pattern (and perhaps to both) of a certain kind of rural society.

However, a case study of two communities in Israel should warn against hasty generalizations: it describes two kibbutzim which share traditions and many common problems yet have chosen drastically different methods for the settlement of legal conflicts.[38] An evaluation of the out-of-court accommodation in present-day Communist China is particularly difficult. In the quite recent past foreign observers and, until the anti-Confucian campaign began, also some Chinese Communists were impressed by an apparent similarity between the present-day insistence on mediation and Confucian traditions. Both admonish people to shun courts, and both are critical of any subjective rights accrued to individuals. But there is new evidence, confirmed by the Maoist leadership, that the mediation now resorted to has completely transformed traditional ways of settling disputes. Individual mediators and special mediation committees no longer count on voluntary compromise or passive submission to third-party recommendations. What is expected from the parties to a dispute is their active "mobilization" in line with the material and ideological demands of the party leadership.[39] In the end this amounts to a reintroduction of judicial decision-making by public authorities even though it still takes place outside of the court system.

In the industrialized societies of the West out-of-court settlements

---

[36] This practice is reported by Northrop, 1959, p. 185.

[37] See Weiner, 1965, p. 214.

[38] As quoted by Becker, 1970, pp. 104ff.

[39] See Lubman, 1967, pp. 1284ff.

are far more frequent than is sometimes realized. A reliable study conducted some time ago in New Haven concluded that more than 80 percent of all disputes arising out of accidents and contractual relationships are settled without a trial. American and European judges are known to favor such a solution not only because of an overload of cases but whenever they fear that certain protracted controversies might endanger the desirable cohesion of the profession.[40] (On the practice of plea-bargaining as an instance of a covert out-of-court settlement, see above, Chapter 5.)

Commercial arbitration was known in Europe in premodern times. French businessmen had concluded early that legally trained judges would be unfit to evaluate the subtle understandings by which the business community lived. Today many groups and subsystems in Western society, among them the professions, are anxious to settle disputes arising between their members through private channels and by agencies they have set up themselves. The government neither can nor wishes to interfere with these private legal systems which keep a substantial amount of litigation out of the courts. Groups and associations create their own norms and interpret and administer them, usually as they see fit. When conflicts arise they take over adjudication so that they are legislators, parties, judge, jury, and police, all in one.[41]

In France the possibilities of resorting to arbitration are more strictly limited than elsewhere. In a country where the image of the state looms larger than for instance in Great Britain and the United States, no dispute that involves an element of "public order" can be settled outside of the regular courts. An appeal to the courts from an arbitration award is always possible even if the parties had specifically agreed on binding arbitration.

In general giant corporations will submit the disputes arising between them, or between them and public authorities, to the regular court system only when they cannot help it. The larger the economic interests involved, the greater the likelihood that settlement will be by mediation or arbitration to which the parties have usually agreed beforehand. Such procedures are at least functionally quite similar to the arbitration to which state enterprises in the Soviet Union have recourse. There too thousands of disputes are settled annually not by the Soviet courts, but by commissions composed of both jurists and technicians.

When they engage in adjudication of disputes, the private legal systems in the Western democracies resort to their own views of "natural justice." Those who lack power and influence may find themselves enmeshed in procedures resembling a kangaroo court. Their remonstrations

---

[40] For opinions by German judges see Weyrauch, 1964, p. 222.

[41] On law-making and adjudication by private groups see Jaffe, 1937, pp. 201–53, and the extensive literature cited there.

will frequently be answered by the claim that, given the demonstrable inefficiency of the courts, the subsystems engage in nothing more than a form of judicial self-help. But that's what lynching also is.

Without close public scrutiny and control certain methods of out-of-court settlement may therefore, in spite of their advantages, result in serious dangers to the commonweal.

ADMINISTRATIVE TRIBUNALS

Mediation and arbitration are designed to avoid the interference of the public court system with litigation which, according to at least one of the parties involved, is better dealt with elsewhere. The question of whether another species of conflicts, namely those arising between the citizen and the public authorities, are best settled by the ordinary courts or by a particular kind of "arbitration" has long been in dispute between different legal systems. What is undisputed is a growing awareness that in modern society conflicts of this kind are becoming ever more numerous and that they may involve the weightiest issues to be decided by the community. What is at stake is an all but universal problem: how can the government be entrusted with the substantial amount of discretion which it needs to function effectively and at the same time how can the citizens' rights be protected against that discretion?

In their search for an answer the civil-law and common-law cultures have started from seemingly opposite basic assumptions and have, until quite recently, engaged in lengthy polemics about the respective virtues of the solution advocated by each side. Differences in outlook, partly historically grounded, partly ideological, have had their impact on the development of institutions for this particular kind of conflict settlement. The distinction, and at times dichotomy, between public and private law has a long history in the civil-law tradition.[42] In England, on the other hand, Lord Coke in his fight with the monarchy imposed the view that all royal acts and privileges were subject to the scrutiny of the common-law courts. Moreover the fact that it was always the king and the royal writs, issued in his name by the judges, that decided the conflicts brought to court, emphasized the public character of all trials, whoever the parties might be.

On the continent the French Revolution and the rising middle class found it quite advantageous to freeze the distinction bequeathed to them by the Roman law. The sphere of private law and above all the rules regulating property or, for the propertyless, those disposing of their labor, were considered immune to governmental interference. In this realm the

[42] Merryman, 1969, p. 99.

state was supposedly neutral; its courts were assigned the role of enforcing private rights based on property or contract. But questions involving
the acts by public authorities had to be dealt with differently. A French
law of 1790, quite in line with the generalized distrust of the professional
judiciary, warned the judges against meddling with the business of government as carried on by the political executive under the responsibility of
the elected assembly. Yet safeguards were deemed necessary against the
revival of too vast an amount of absolute discretion which in the name of
the state would interfere with the interests of the bourgeoisie. In the
constitution of 1799 Napoleon found the appropriate compromise. "I want
to create," as he put it,

> *a half-administrative, half-judicial body which should reflect that part of
> discretion which is indispensable for the administration of the state. To
> leave that discretion in the hands of the Prince [that is, the Executive] is
> inadvisable for he would either exercise it badly or neglect to exercise it
> altogether.*[43]

The Council of State which was then established has survived many
a political storm and has remained the apex of a hierarchy of administrative tribunals. Its members are not judges "like the others." (There are
about eighty in the Litigation Section which alone interests us here, though
the Council has other functions too.) The Councillors of State, legally
trained though they may be, form one of the highly respected *corps* of
civil servants whose prestige has at all times outranked that of the ordinary
judges. Since the war most of them are the top graduate of the National
School of Administration where they have been trained, together with
other future *grands fonctionnaires,* in a broad field of administrative sciences, rather than in civil or criminal law.

The Council and the administrative tribunals under its purview (all
manned by civil servants) are competent to adjudicate all conflicts in
which public authorities of whatever level are involved. The landmark
decisions of the Council have built an imposing body of administrative case
law quite in the manner of a court in a common-law system. They have
protected the citizens' civil rights as well as their pecuniary interests against
either the arbitrariness or merely the errors of officialdom. When they find
that the executive has overstepped its bounds or is otherwise at fault, they
annul administrative acts and may award damages to injured citizens.

In most countries of continental Europe the French Council of State

---

[43] Kessler, 1968, p. 28. This is an excellent up-to-date monograph on the Council
of State. For a good discussion of the Council of State in English, see Abraham,
1968, pp. 269ff.

has earned the highest admiration. With some variations, the French model of a hierarchy of administrative tribunals was emulated in many lands. In nineteenth-century England the very concept of administrative law and of special administrative courts was considered anathema, violative of the principle that nobody could be a judge in his own case and thoroughly alien to the spirit of the common law. Albert Dicey's at one time quite influential treatise *Introduction to the Study of the Law of the Constitution* (1885) maintained, as Lord Coke had argued in a vastly different political setting, that there could be only one law to which all, government and governed alike, were subject. His misreading of the continental record coupled with an idealized mixture of the judicial process in common-law countries emboldened him to see in administrative courts a gateway to tyranny and a betrayal of the rule of law. The inconsistencies of Dicey's position even in his own time have often been pointed out; [44] since the time when he wrote, administrative reality in all common-law countries has ignored his warnings. Yet among English and American lawyers there probably still survive some lingering beliefs "that to the courts alone had been granted an understanding of the mysteries of objectivity and impartiality." [45]

If nothing else the growth of the social-service state in all modern countries has made the organization of administrative tribunals of various kinds indispensable. It became clear that ordinary court procedures were far too lengthy, costly, and often inappropriate because of an insufficient expertise of the judges to adjudicate conflicts arising from the multitude of administrative decisions. In Great Britain the acquisition of judicial powers by administrative tribunals has been called one of the most striking developments of constitutional life. Not less than 2,000 "special tribunals" exist; they handle far more cases than the ordinary courts and their impact on ordinary citizens, on associations, and on firms of all kinds, is far greater than that of the courts.[46] In the United States decisions by a host of administrative tribunals and regulatory agencies penetrate most aspects of economic and social life. In both Great Britain and the United States as well as in other common-law countries access to these tribunals is easier and cheaper than to the courts; their proceedings are not bound by the formalities of the courts, and their rules for the gathering of evidence are far less restrictive.

[44] For a critical discussion of Dicey's arguments, see Friedmann, 1972, pp. 379ff. and the authors quoted there.

[45] Abel-Smith and Stevens, 1968, p. 229.

[46] For an illuminating discussion of the activities of administrative tribunals in England, see Jackson, 1967, pp. 351–469 (the entire Chapter 6, entitled "Special Tribunals").

These and similar developments have considerably narrowed the gap that existed in this field between civil-law and common-law countries not too many decades ago. No country can claim to have found a solution which will always combine administrative efficiency with all the necessary safeguards for the rights and interests of the governed. On the cardinal problem of how to guarantee the utmost objectivity, judiciousness, and fairness in administrative adjudication, different views continue to determine the structure and operation of existing institutions. Most European and some Latin American countries continue to put their faith in a hierarchy of administrative courts, fairly insulated from the regular court system and manned usually by specially trained civil servants. In postwar France, the Council of State manifested its independence and steadfastness when it struck down certain extravagancies of the Gaullist regime considered as unnecessary and possibly dangerous infringements of civil rights. In addition to its many other tasks the Prokuratura in the Soviet Union also acts as a censor of administrative irregularities; it has therefore been cited as being functionally akin to the French Council of State. British and American occupation authorities had insisted that West Germany strengthen the prerogatives of its administrative courts so as to guarantee the respect for the rule of law; this appears somewhat ironical in view of the fact that neither England nor the United States has chosen this pattern of control in their own countries.

In common-law countries the creation of a complete hierarchy of administrative courts has been shunned. There continue to exist a somewhat bewildering array of boards, commissions, and tribunals which all dispense "justice" but whose membership varies according to the subject matter they have to deal with. There exist possibilities for appeal either to other tribunals and, in many though not in all cases, to the general courts. One may therefore speak of a compromise solution between the earlier notions of the common law and the needs of a bureaucratic age. For the U.S. Supreme Court the review of administrative action has become its single most important activity: about one-third of its full-opinion cases are concerned with such matters, while questions of constitutional law proper are decided in only one-fourth of the cases with which the Supreme Court has to deal. What has clearly moved into the foreground of concern in all legal systems is the possibility of striking down the obnoxious and arbitrary misuse of administrative discretion. Who exercises this control is a question of secondary importance.

In recent years the ombudsman—first instituted in Sweden early in the nineteenth century—has met with widespread interest. Many legal systems are experimenting at various levels with an adaptation of this office as a supplement rather than as an alternative to the system of administrative justice. The methods used and the extent of ombudsman's power vary from country to country, since the institution is not easily transferred from one constitutional framework to another. In countries such as France which has a full-fledged system of administrative justice, many felt that an additional organ for the protection of the rights of the individual was unnecessary. So far the experience has not been regarded as a full success and was also opposed by certain members of parliament who saw themselves deprived of yet another of their functions, that of protecting their constituents, the *administrés*, against the bureaucracy. In the United Kingdom similar reserves on the part of the Members of Parliament limited the functions of the newly established office of a Parliamentary Commissioner for Administration. In contrast it appears that in New Zealand and in one socialist country, Yugoslavia, an official very similar to the Scandinavian ombudsman is engaging in rather extensive and successful activities. In Canada and in the United States experimentation is still going forward on both the federal and the state provincial level.

In general the emergence of the institution has rightly been regarded as a "symbol of the demands for new modes of redress against a large and opaque government apparatus." [47] Where the ombudsman has been most effective, he has been concerned not so much with general administrative principles as with specific citizens' grievances which often arise from an inequitable rather than an abusive or illegal application of laws and regulations. The fact that the ombudsman himself is not restricted to basing his recommendations on legal provisions, but instead might put forward equitable considerations, is a recognition of the limits of law in a complicated society.

---

[47] Selznick, 1968, p. 54. See also Friedmann, 1972, pp. 438–41, and for a comparative yet already slightly obsolete survey, see Gellhorn, 1966.

THE LIMITS OF LAW

7

THE IMPACT OF COURTS

Previous parts of this study have shown that in many situations no clear dividing line exists between rule-making and rule application. As we have seen, the true content of a norm is not definitely determined by the wording given to it by a precedent or by a statute, but by the fate it meets in the judicial (or the administrative) process. The Law is made, in the often quoted phrase of Jeremy Bentham, by Judge and Company. Yet even when judge or administrator have spoken and thereby made their contribution to policy output, the outcome is not necessarily decided. We must "ask ourselves what happens after the judicial decision has been rendered. A good romantic novel ends with a marriage. But sometimes the tragedy starts just afterwards." [1] To take but one striking example from a book significantly entitled *Law, the Science of Inefficiency*: during a given period not more than 7 percent of all money judgments in New York County were collected by the seemingly successful party. [2] To gauge the true, as opposed to the assumed, effects of law on the rest of life we will need "mazes of informal data and multiplied cause-effect relations." [3]

In the United States increasing attention has been paid of late to the problem of compliance with court rulings and thereby to their actual impact on society. What one author, investigating the effect of Supreme Court decisions on religious practices in public schools, has called the "dynamics of compliance" results in considerable variations concerning the ability of law to enforce standards of behavior. [4] While the findings avail-

[1] Pekelis, 1950, pp. 44f.

[2] Seagle, 1952, p. 3.

[3] Hurst, 1971, p. 67.

[4] Johnson, 1967.

able to date are based almost exclusively on Supreme Court decisions, reasonable hopes are expressed that at least some of the variables that have been identified may also prove of value for impact studies of other United States courts.[5]

The style and the language of a decision might make a difference for compliance: whether its wording is clear or, perhaps deliberately, ambiguous; whether the judges have indicated, as they tried to do in the first school desegregation cases, how their decision should be implemented; how many judges participated in the majority decision; and how persuasive the dissents are. Of great importance is the economic, social, and political situation into which the decision has injected itself. One writer has concluded, not surprisingly, that when the U.S. Supreme Court moves as an integral part of the dominant national alliance, its decisions might indeed set or confirm policies, but when it feels compelled to act, as it were, alone, its impact might be next to nil.[6] On the other hand, when there is a stalemate between the other branches of government, decisions by the Court will be welcome as offering an escape from responsibility. In fairly recent times the Court has had such matters as desegregation and the reform of criminal procedures largely to itself.

The attitudes of government officials, beginning with the President or a Governor down to the local school board or the police precinct station make a difference in the impact which a ringing Supreme Court decision has in the nation or in a given community.[7] In order to be effective all courts must frequently engage in coalition politics with those who hold the key to compliance; in the process they will weigh the short-range results that can be expected from restrained enforcement against the risks of insisting on more direct, hence more political, and by the same token more risky long-range goals.[8] On their part, both the officials in charge of enforcement and the individuals or organizations to which the court decision is addressed might evaluate the ratio between costs and benefits to be expected from compliance or noncompliance, partial or total; they will then act according to this calculation.

It seems to be quite generally true that there exists an upper limit of effectiveness for enforcement resources; beyond that limit additional

---

[5] For an extensive and interesting discussion of the literature on legal impact see Wasby, 1973, and Grossman and Sarat, 1971, pp. 177ff.

[6] So claims Dahl, 1967, pp 167ff., with some striking examples.

[7] Note the remark by the N.Y. City Police Commissioner characterizing the alleged fact that Supreme Court decisions play a role in the day-to-day operation of a major police department as "close to a myth," *New York Times*, July 29, 1973, p. 31.

[8] See Ulmer, 1971, pp. 23ff., for a full discussion of the Supreme Court's tactics for the enforcement of the desegregation decisions.

coercion is either unavailable or ineffective.[9] These and similar findings point to the fact that impact studies ought to be fitted into a larger investigation of the relationship between law and social change. The enforcement history of the desegregation and of the reapportionment decisions by the Supreme Court and by the District Courts indicates that the more people are emotionally involved in the behavior which the law tries to change, the more difficult it will be to obtain effective compliance.

The conclusions which have been drawn from studies of Supreme Court decisions are useful in as much as they elucidate the relationship between law and the political and cultural environment. They are also tentative because all impact studies, as their authors admit, suffer from severe methodological difficulties; even when social changes occur in fields in which the Court has ruled, it might still be open to question whether such changes were coincidental or consequentially related to the ruling.

It appears that so far no studies of this kind have been undertaken in other legal systems. Hence no comparisons between different cultures can be attempted. It is not unlikely that the problems and difficulties of enforcement which have been identified in the United States have their equivalent in other countries, at least as far as decisions by their highest courts are concerned. There is in fact a striking similarity between the controversies with which some of these courts have had to deal since the Second World War. In Australia, Canada, and in West Germany, issues of federalism, free speech, and freedom of political association have frequently come before the courts; in Ireland and in Japan problems of criminal justice and in Ireland and Germany the governmental control of education were the subjects of several searching decisions; legislative districting and reapportionment have preoccupied the high courts of Canada, Switzerland, Ireland, Japan, and again of Germany.[10] Similar issues, raised in countries of roughly equal development with certain shared cultural traditions, may be expected to lead to similar problems of enforcement. But the confirmation of such a hypothesis must await the needed research. Ultimately, studies that want to determine the actual impact of law in any society will have to reach farther down and not content themselves with inquiries into the fate of decisions by the highest court.[11]

Authoritarian regimes are wont to claim that "their will be done" and that their every norm, set either by the legislator or by the court, will produce the desired behavior. Since sanctions are more drastic and more readily available, those concerned might evaluate the costs or benefits of compliance

---

[9] See, also for what follows in the text, Barkun, 1971, pp. 3ff.

[10] See Murphy and Tanenhaus, 1972, pp. 31ff.

[11] This is, of course, the task of legal sociology. On the shortcomings of such studies at present, see Selznick, 1968, p. 58.

and noncompliance differently from citizens and officials in a democracy. But the basic problems are the same: it may well be doubted that in the far reaches of the Soviet Union or of China the impact of legal rulings will be uniform and complete.

COURTS AND POLITICS

Courts cannot help playing a part in setting policies. In doing so, they must react, as other branches of the government do, to "the felt necessities of the time," as Justice Holmes put it. But if courts must participate in policy-making and thereby in politics, what are the conditions that permit politics to invade the judicial space and the courts' output? An answer to this question will obviously depend less on a country's legal culture than on the nature of the regime and on the prevailing political situation.

No regime can, without risk to its own survival, tolerate for long a judiciary whose decisions interfere constantly and deliberately with governmental policy. Normally, as we have seen (see above, Chapter 4), the processes of socialization will be enough to keep the professional judiciary in line. The mutual interest of all officeholders in strengthening rather than weakening the legitimacy of the existing order will make direct interference with the activities of the courts unnecessary. Even when there is momentary conflict, the judiciary knows that it has to retreat before the combined and clearly manifested intentions of legislature and executive. President Roosevelt's struggle with the Supreme Court ended with a compromise that ultimately gave way to the somewhat altered policy designs of Congress and President. To be sure, the judiciary leaves its marks on the outcome of such struggles; but it can hardly emerge victorious. Even where the courts have the prerogative of judicial review, a determined legislature can redraft legislation to meet objections raised by the courts, without changing the substance of its program. The difficulties which court orders are likely to meet in the enforcement phase enlarge the power of the political departments, possibly at considerable cost to the judicial.

In order to avoid open conflict which might arise out of fundamental divergencies and yet to save the courts' faith, the judiciary has developed in many countries functionally similar techniques. In the United States the courts will not decide what they term "political questions." Since obviously courts do decide some weighty policy problems, the "political question doctrine" gives the judiciary discretionary powers to determine the extent of its own involvement. What is less a doctrine than an act of judicial statesmanship creates quite deliberately loopholes through which unfettered state power takes over decision-making in a specific domain, as for instance that of foreign policy. The U.S. Supreme Court has an additional escape hatch in its prerogative to refuse *certiorari* to cases which it is unwilling to handle. Paramount problems of public life, such as the recent war in Vietnam, can thereby be shielded from judicial scrutiny. The rationalization for such self-restraint is the insight that in such matters a legal dictum would not affect reality one way or the other, but possibly would sap the foundations of judicial power which remains indispensable for the community in other matters, especially during and after a national crisis.

Where, on the other hand, the judiciary intends and is able to impose views which are in important respects contrary to officially adopted policies, the regime is in serious danger and may falter. This occurred both in the Weimar Republic and in Allende's Chile. In both cases the government lacked either the resources or the will to bend the attitudes of the judiciary in criminal as well as civil trials—one of the reasons for the downfall of these republics.

It is unavoidable that all emergencies result in increased political pressures on the judicial space. Whether the emergency is caused by internal tensions, by foreign threat, or by war, or whether or not constitution or legislation have attempted to spell out the legal consequences of such special circumstances, it is always likely that standards developed in normal times to guarantee rights and privileges will not be upheld. A German constitutional lawyer once stated, long before he became a Nazi, that sovereign is he who decides the emergency situation. Measured by this test the judiciary cannot be sovereign. But while it will have to adjust its decisions in some ways to the demands of the political situation, it does not have to renounce altogether its traditional role.

When President Truman, at the height of the Korean war, seized steel mills which were threatened by strikes and lockouts, the brief which he submitted to the Supreme Court specifically stated that according to his findings a national catastrophy threatened. The Court rescinded the presidential action as violating the constitution and infringing upon congressional prerogatives. Although it did not deny that an emergency existed, the Court was unwilling to "suit the political conveniences" arising from the situation.[12] During the cold war public-opinion polls showed that about 80 percent of the people in the United States, in Canada, and in Australia were in favor of outlawing their national Communist parties. Nonetheless the high courts in these countries invalidated all or part of the legislation designed to dissolve Communist organizations.[13]

Comparative inquiries into the way the courts of various systems have reacted to a state of emergency offer ample materials for an understanding

[12] See Youngstown Sheet and Tube Company v. Sawyer, 343 U.S. 579 (1952).
[13] See Becker, 1970, p. 230.

of the limits which politics impose on judicial values and on law itself.[14]

A dictatorship accepts nothing less than the total integration of the courts within the policy goals of the government. Most of the time this does not preclude an adherence to the formalistic characteristics of law and court procedures. But when the regime feels threatened or wants to give the appearance that a threat exists, the courts become the instruments of sheer terror. This happened at various times in the Soviet Union, especially during the purge trials of the Stalin years, and in Nazi Germany when "enemies of the state" were prosecuted before special courts.

Yet political trials, where politics and law are interlocked in a special way, are not confined to dictatorships. Political justice has been defined by the foremost student of the phenomenon as "the use of the judicial process for the purpose of gaining (or upholding or enlarging) or limiting (or destroying) political power or influence." [15]

The courts are then called upon to assume an active role in political strife; the law is used to eliminate those who oppose the regime or at least to make them powerless. The nature of the opposition, the traditional role of legal and constitutional guarantees, and also an imminent stability or erosion of the regime will generally determine the forms and outcomes of the trials. The number of political trials throughout history, their recurrent and occasionally novel themes—from Socrates and Joan of Arc to Captain Dreyfus, Sacco and Vanzetti, and the Harrisburg Seven—make their investigation another rewarding subject for comparative studies.[16]

JUDICIAL REVIEW

The authority of a court to declare laws and official acts unconstitutional is a practice which sheds a strong light on the interplay of law and politics. It is a judicial act which gives to judges so obvious a share in policy-making that where it prevails there is little room left for the pretense that judges only apply the law (even though Justice Marshall engaged in just such a pretense in Marbury v. Madison). Judicial refusal to apply a law and the extent and the scope of the authority to do so have been regarded as indicators of independence. The questions of why such a guardianship of the fundamental law is entrusted to the judiciary in some systems and denied in others, and what are the reasons—frequently divergent

---

[14] This has been attempted by Rossiter, 1948, in an excellent but by now somewhat dated comparative study. For a study dealing only with recent American experiences but viewed from a comparative perspective see Kommers, 1972, pp. 603–28.

[15] Kirchheimer, 1961, pp. 425ff. and passim.

[16] Becker, 1971, has presented, together with case studies of political trials in nine countries, an interesting classification of such trials which should help further comparisons.

—justifying judicial review, are all critical problems for the place and the function of law and of courts in the political system.

The fact that almost one-half of the nations of the world have by now officially adopted some form of judicial review invites meaningful comparisons. In many countries this is a very recent development and frequently actual practice does not conform to what the constitutions promise. What emerges from studies undertaken so far, whether monographic or comparative, is an impression that neither cultural traditions, nor the forms of government, nor the conscious desire to emulate foreign examples or to draw lessons from past experiences can be regarded as *single* causes for different practices and for the philosophies connected with these practices.[17] It is true that, just as in the United States, judicial review has found more ready acceptance in common-law countries; but Great Britain has never conceded its courts this power, while by now many civil-law countries on all continents have accepted it, some with great success. Although federalism seems to invite using judicial review as a method of umpiring the nation-state relationship, there are federal systems such as the Soviet Union which frown on it while unitary systems such as Japan and many of the developing countries have introduced or at least promised it. Authoritarian one-party systems are generally disinclined to give such powers to their judiciary; but Yugoslavia allows a broad constitutional review to a special Constitutional Court. Whereas some countries insist that the institution can and must be justified by positive commands of constitutional law or ordinary legislation, others wish to base it at least in part on an old or renewed commitment to natural law.

If no single factor can provide an explanation, a combination of circumstances will determine the existence, forms, and content of the power to review. This amounts to saying that this is another field where different legal cultures have adopted a similar though not always identical institution and that, once adopted, judicial review prospers or fails in response to many influences. For reasons of space and because many additional studies will be necessary, the observations which follow do not attempt a systematic survey of a widespread constitutional development. They merely wish to evaluate whether and to what extent attitudes by and toward the judiciary (as discussed in previous chapters) provide at least a partial explanation of existing differences. This also should elicit further the mutual impact of law and politics and hence the limits of law, especially in those countries on whose legal cultures we have frequently commented.

On the basis of historical experiences in the United States it is sometimes postulated that without judicial review there can be no truly inde-

---

[17] Kommers, 1975, pp. 282ff., comments on a great number of these studies in helpful systematic fashion. Interesting also is the survey by Cappelletti and Adams, 1966, pp. 1,207ff.

pendent judiciary. There are a number of Western democracies, known for steadfast liberal traditions, which belie such a claim; among them are Belgium, Denmark, and Switzerland (the latter as regards federal legislation). Norwegian and Swedish courts have the power to review, but they never use it.

The case of Great Britain deserves special discussion. Even though it has no written constitution, it does have a constitution whose binding standards have been evolved by custom and convention and which could serve as a yardstick for the "constitutionality" of legislation and administrative acts. Indeed the common law adheres to the very idea of a higher law on which all judicial review is based.[18] Nevertheless the legislative output of the British Parliament cannot be invalidated by the courts; acts by the executive and its organs can at best be censured indirectly before administrative tribunals. But the inability to erase does not prevent authoritative interpretation. The British courts, and especially those of last instance, have imposed their principled views on important statutory enactments, among them those concerned with civil liberties, property rights, and the most varied kinds of human relationships. Should their interpretation be out of step with the state of public opinion for a protracted time, Parliament can legislate again on the subject and it will usually do so in a way that does not risk interference from the courts. But this only shows that courts do "interfere," when they find it opportune to do so, and as long as they can.

It is sometimes said that in the United States it would take a constitutional amendment to change a court ruling, where in England a simple law is sufficient. But also in the United States some form of judicial self-restraint will usually prevent the judges from dealing too harshly with legislation. Except in extraordinary situations, outright invalidations are rare. Within a somewhat smaller compass the problems of balancing fundamental principles against widely approved policy designs are much the same for British and American courts. One of the foremost students of comparative judicial review has appropriately suggested that the British courts exercise "indirect judicial review."[19] Their interpretation, narrowing or broadening the meaning of a statute in order to brake what the judges consider an undesirable excess, applies a technique far more frequently used by the U.S. Supreme Court than that of nullifying legislation.

The record of the British judiciary for independence, especially in regard to executive acts encroaching upon civil liberties during emergencies created by wars, hot or cold, has been at least equal to that of American courts.[20] As a matter of fact, the less political, if highly elitist, selection of

---

[18] See Corwin (1928–29), 1959, and McIlwain, 1947.

[19] McWhinney, 1965, p. 13.

[20] For an often quoted example see the majority and minority opinions in Liversidge v. Anderson (1942) A. C. 206.

English judges appears to guarantee a great amount of independence. In addition, the point has been made that the somewhat more limited checks available to the British judges have preserved them from the ideological warfare into which the U.S. Supreme Court has occasionally been drawn and which has proved detrimental to the independence of the American judiciary.[21] It therefore appears correct to conclude that "the presence or absence of judicial review, whether legally or in practice, is only one (and perhaps not the most convincing) indicator of the degree of judicial independence extant in a culture." [22]

The emergence of judicial review in British Commonwealth countries lends itself to a variety of explanations, but a concern for judicial independence is not among them since such an independence was achieved well before the high courts of these countries started to review the constitutionality of legislation.[23] The Privy Council's right to review upon appeal cases decided by the Dominion courts had accustomed the members of the Commonwealth to interpretations of their constitutional laws by an umpire. Hence when the Privy Council lost these prerogatives, the Supreme Courts of the Commonwealth nations were more amenable to the practices of direct judicial review than the British House of Lords. The fact that judicial review is particularly prevalent in Canada and Australia gives credence to the sometimes overstressed fact that the institution is apt to prosper in federally organized states.

Undoubtedly, the Supreme Courts of both countries have come close to amending their respective constitutions and have helped in rearranging relationships between the federal governments and their constituent units. The British North America Act of 1867 had intended to strengthen the federal authority in Ottawa, but over the years powers have shifted from the center to the provinces so that during the depression the so-called Canadian New Deal legislation was invalidated on the ground that it interfered with the exclusive powers of the provinces to legislate in relation to property. What first the Privy Council and later the Supreme Court of Canada sanctioned were economic and cultural developments originating in French-speaking Quebec and in western Canada.

The Australian High Court has exercised its review powers in a way characteristic of majority opinions of the U.S. Supreme Court during two distinct periods. In the economic sphere it has come down in general on the side of freedom from state regulation and laissez faire. In the field of civil liberties the High Court has constantly construed all legislation interfering

---

[21] According to Friedmann, 1967, p. 449.

[22] Becker, 1970, p. 213.

[23] For extensive comments, see McWhinney, 1965, pp. 96–126. The author also reports on interesting developments in India, Pakistan, and South Africa, which for reasons of space cannot be discussed here.

with the full exercise of such rights as narrowly as possible. Moreover it has done so not with any reference to a higher moral order, but by insisting, as their English brethren would, that they were only giving a reasonable interpretation to the wording of statutes.

The case of Ireland is significantly different. After the country had won independence, its constitution explicitly provided for the invalidation of legislation by the courts. In fact to date no Irish court has availed itself of this right. The fact that Ireland has lived for about thirty years in a state of emergency and the not very exalted status of Irish judges appear to be the foremost reasons for such an extreme form of judicial self-restraint.

During the postwar years, when in neighboring countries judicial review began to blossom, the scrutiny of cantonal legislation by the Swiss Federal Court receded. The Court never had the power to review the constitutionality of federal law. But after the war its judges, whose careers became in substance if not in form more and more assimilated to that of civil servants (see above, Chapter 4), also left cantonal laws largely untouched. In an age of rapidly expanding governmental services, both federal and cantonal, Swiss judges were fully aware of the political character of most legislative enactments. Hence strong traditions to reserve political decisions to the legislatures and to the frequent popular referendums have asserted themselves.[24]

The experiences of the three former Axis powers with judicial review are particularly noteworthy. In abiding by civil-law traditions all of them had rejected the institution in the past, except that during the Weimar Republic antidemocratic judges had sought to introduce judicial scrutiny of socially progressive legislation through the back door. When a jurist in postwar Italy stated that his country felt "the impact of Marbury v. Madison almost a century and a half after the decision,"[25] he pointed correctly to the conscious imitation of the United States model on the part of all three nations. This had not been true in the case of the Commonwealth countries. But in West Germany and in Japan the occupation authorities had urged the introduction of judicial review as a way of promoting the democratic way of life.

While Japan has adopted the American pattern of granting review powers to its Supreme Court, both West Germany and Italy have created special Constitutional Courts. They thereby follow a recent trend of European systems to create special courts in different legal realms which emphasize the expertise of specialists. Most of the members of the German and Italian Constitutional Courts are particularly versed in problems of public

[24] See Morrison, 1969, pp. 133–62.
[25] Quoted by Cole, 1959, p. 967.

law. Considering that judicial review had been largely unknown in Germany, its new Court has been unusually successful in terms of prestige, of output, and even of impact. The general population has only a vague image of the Court's activities, but the same is true of the image of the U.S. Supreme Court (see above, Chapter 4). However, 90 percent of the legal and political elites in the German Federal Republic consider the exercise of judicial review powers by the court indispensable, or at least highly useful, for "democracy." [26]

The West German Constitutional Court's two chambers have decided thousands of cases, two-thirds of them complaints by citizens about a violation of constitutional rights. The other cases usually concerned disputes between organs of federal or state governments, the Court acting here frequently, like its United States equivalent, as the federal umpire. Expressed in mere numbers the amount of either federal or state statutes which the Court has declared unconstitutional has been characterized as "judicial activism run wild." [27] In a few instances the Court has actually compelled the executive or parliament to modify or change major policies. However, most of the nullified statutes have been of minor importance and, as in other countries, judicial review in West Germany has fulfilled the function of legitimizing the political system. According to reports the rate of compliance with the Court's rulings has been high. To explain the overall success of the Court, the conclusion which one of its foremost American students has put forward is entirely warranted: "the [West German] system is sufficiently bi-partisan, federal and pluralistic in character to enable the Court to win support among power centers and important political groupings in and out of government." [28] This points correctly to the intimate connection between legal and political factors that have facilitated the acclimatization of the institution in a foreign soil.

In addition a revival of thinking about natural law among German jurists in general and among the judges on the Court in particular is noteworthy. The natural-law tradition, the belief that there exist higher principles on which all law should orient itself, has been germane to German jurisprudential thinking even though it has at times run more under than above ground. A totalitarian regime such as Germany has experienced is always brutally positivistic; in its eyes "an order is an order no matter what." As a reaction against the Nazi concepts a return to natural law seemed desirable: it has encouraged the judges on the Court to examine whether legislative and executive acts conform to the basic values of society and

[26] See Kommers, 1970, pp. 8ff., also for a comparison of the German and Italian courts.

[27] Kommers, 1969, p. 113.

[28] Kommers, 1970, p. 24.

polity. This could have lead to a judicialization of political life and to an undesirable paramountcy of the judiciary. But at least so far this has not been the case, which is another indication that luckily the post–World War I and post–World War II German republics are of a different kind.

The Italian Constitutional Court has not been similarly successful. The fact that eight years elapsed between the promulgation of the postwar constitution that had announced the introduction of judicial review and the actual organization of the Court bespeaks the hesitations of civil-law trained jurists. Many doubted the suitability and even the legitimacy of a judicial review of legislation. After the Court started functioning the judges moved with considerable caution: in the field of criminal proceedings they have struck down most remnants of the fascist era; they have established some principles concerning the exercise of the privilege of free speech within the rather narrow limits granted to it in present-day Italy. When called upon to decide issues of regionalism, the mild form of federalism that is being tried out in Italy, the court has usually come out in favor of traditional centralization.

Spotty compliance with the Court's rulings by parliament and, on the local level, by the police can at least in part be traced to the tentative and mostly hortatory language of the decisions. Some judges claim that the mere existence of the Court has prevented parliamentary excesses. But altogether the Court has not bid for that share of political influence which the constitution seemed to make possible.[29] A continuing distrust of anything resembling sweeping judicial creativity can in part be explained by traditions. It also expresses a reluctance to increase the tensions which uncertain political coalitions have created and which threaten the regime's and therewith the Court's legitimacy.

The Japanese Supreme Court has also used its U.S.-imposed authority quite sparingly to review the constitutionality of legislation. In a culture which still prefers dispute settlement outside of the courts, the apex of the judicial hierarchy encounters difficulties in acquiring the social and political weight that is needed for effective judicial review. If the visibility and the prestige of the Court have increased slowly since 1947, this is in part due to the important role which the Court is playing in the nomination of judges (see above, Chapter 4). At least indirectly this also seems to have affected the Court's constitutional review powers.

For years the judges used an equivalent of the American "political question doctrine" (see above) when refusing to strike down any legislation. The first three cases which invalidated some statutes were devoid of any practical significance. Only in 1973, a quarter of a century after the Supreme Court had been granted its novel authority, was an at least sym-

---

[29] For an overall evaluation of the Italian practice see Bognetti, 1973.

bolically important provision of the Penal Code declared unconstitutional. The Code had prescribed heavier penalties for parricide, that is, in cases of murder where the victims were lineal ascendants. This, the Court declared, was a violation of the equality principle proclaimed by the constitution.[30] While the Minister of Justice and the prosecuting authorities promised compliance with the decision, which conservatives considered a blow to traditional notions, it will not be easy to evaluate the actual effect of the ruling on convictions in lower courts. Whether this new departure in the exercise of the Court's review power will extend to other fields will depend not only on political developments but also on the attitudes of the generation of Japanese judges who are now reaching the top level.

Special circumstances of totalitarianism and its defeat explain why judicial review has found its way into three countries belonging to the civil-law world. Some of the basic concepts and traditions of the civil-law systems as well as some practical considerations have long been inimical to the practice of judicial review by either their ordinary courts or by a special constitutional court. Strictly speaking the exercise of review power is incompatible with the dogma of a sharp separation between legislative and judicial power.[31] We have seen why the French revolutionaries wished to establish and maintain such a separation; at least on the level of theoretical commitment many civil-law countries have followed the French example.

In France the ephemeral status of many of its constitutions was compensated for by the elevation of any law, adopted by parliament, as the true and only expression of the general will and of popular sovereignty. But this concept defeats the very basis for differentiation between constitutional law and ordinary laws: the former cannot control the content of the latter. Another argument which has found its way into some of the decisions of the Council of State admits that the law cannot derogate from the constitution since as a matter of principle the latter has legal authority superior to that of a simple statute. But since positive law does not provide a means of asserting that superior authority, and since a principle without sanction cannot be considered a legal principle, the conclusion remains the same: there cannot be judicial control of constitutionality.

When the presidential systems of Latin American countries followed the constitutional pattern of the United States, while remaining otherwise faithful to civil-law traditions, they encountered an additional difficulty. Since to them a decision has no binding force except for the parties in the legal suit before the court, there exist the hazards of inconsistent decisions by different courts; the same statute might be upheld by one court and invalidated by another. This danger has been obviated to a certain extent by

[30] See Danielski, 1969 and 1973.

[31] See Merryman, 1969, p. 25 and, for what follows in the text, pp. 144ff.

giving limited review powers only to the countries' supreme courts, but the results have been generally unsatisfactory. Until the recent suspension of the constitution by the Junta, the Chilean Supreme Court has been generally regarded as being somewhat more forceful than others in the exercise of judicial control of legislation. But even its impact has been close to negligible. The Mexican system knows of a special suit by which ordinary citizens can appeal to the court when the constitution appears violated. However, the courts' authority to declare laws unconstitutional remains limited; that the courts can never interfere with legislation affecting land distribution appears a wise stricture to those who are familiar with the history of Mexican reforms.[32]

Developments in the French Fifth Republic are in some ways congruent with the recent trend toward some form of constitutional review in the civil-law world; in other respects the French experience has been so far deliberately divergent. One of the innovations of the Constitution of 1958 was the institution of a Constitutional Council (Art. 56–62). In addition to a number of other functions the Council may declare void all laws that do not conform to the constitution. A provision declared unconstitutional may not be promulgated nor implemented. The Council's decisions are final and binding on all.

Both access to the Council and its composition have made the Council a political rather than a judicial organ and this in turn determines the nature of its review powers. Except in some special cases where the Council is obligated to take jurisdiction without a request, only the President of the Republic, the Prime Minister, and the Speakers of the upper and the lower house of parliament can bring cases before the Council. No complaints by individuals or groups protesting the violation of constitutional rights are admitted. The nine members on the Council are appointed for nonrenewable nine-year terms by the President and the two speakers. During the first fifteen years of the Republic all of the members have been distinguished and generally respected personalities, but they were selected for political reasons rather than for their legal competence. Some have been lawyers, but none has exercised judicial functions prior to his nomination.

If genuine judicial review infringes necessarily upon the strict separation of powers as understood in France, the French Constitutional Council was entitled and expected, by the nature of the cases brought before it, to become the very guardian of a particular separation of powers which was a core concern of the Gaullist constitution. Many of its decisions limited the powers of parliament in favor of the government's constitutional right to legislate by executive ordinance or decree. Although not all of the Council's decisions have been in favor of the government, it has been regarded as

[32] For the Mexican practice see Baker, 1971, p. 132 and passim.

the watchdog of the executive and its moral authority has, on the whole, remained mediocre. At a dramatic moment of the Fifth Republic, in 1962, the Council was called upon to decide on the constitutionality of a referendum which President de Gaulle had called in violation of the existing provisions for constitutional amendment to alter the method of presidential elections. The Council refused to rule, since a majority of the people had spoken.

First in 1971, and subsequently in two decisions rendered in 1973, the Council started assuming a somewhat different role which has been heralded (or criticized) as the beginning of a new era of constitutional control. In these cases the Council declared unconstitutional a limited number of legislative provisions which directly or indirectly touched upon the rights and privileges of citizens, among them the untrammeled right of association, the equality before fiscal authorities, and the proper form of criminal statutes providing for imprisonment.

When the Council annulled in 1971 certain provisions of a law which the Minister in charge of public order had introduced and which had been approved by the strong Gaullist majority in parliament, it declared that the way in which the law tried to control subversive associations violated the "fundamental principles recognized by the laws of the Republic." According to the Council's decision those principles were incorporated in the preambles to the constitutions of both the Fourth and the Fifth Republics. Some commentators have minimized the importance of the ruling mainly by pointing to the vagueness of the constitutional provisions that had been invoked. Others have seen in the decision the French equivalent of Marbury v. Madison. But unlike the U.S. Supreme Court, the French Council has not waited long years before asserting anew its right to judicial scrutiny of parliamentary legislation. There can be no doubt that the decisions it rendered in 1971 and 1973 have increased the prestige of the Council and have reopened the debate about whether the time has not come to introduce full-fledged judicial review and thereby follow the example recently set by other civil-law countries.

As long as the constitution restricted access to the Council to four officials who all might be close to the government or to the majority in parliament, the Council's review powers could not effectively control the activities of the two other branches of government. This, however, is the essence of judicial review. The president of the French republic elected in 1974, no longer a Gaullist, wished to make larger review powers for the Constitutional Council a matter of priority. It turned out that he lacked the necessary majorities in parliament to obtain all he had hoped for. But the constitutional amendment that was approved stipulated that any sixty members of either house of parliament could now appeal to the Council for its scrutiny of recent legislation. The new arrangement could prove effective for the defense of minority rights and made the intervention by the Council less sporadic. Even though individuals are still barred from appealing to the Council, it is likely that France will move somewhat closer to practices current in neighboring Italy and, above all, in West Germany. Yet the obstacles to overcome are quite considerable, among them a centuries-old tradition of according unlimited sovereignty to laws approved by a majority of the nation's representatives.

The Soviet Union and other Communist countries in Eastern Europe which follow the Russian model deny any review power to their judiciary. They reject the very idea of checks and balances and adhere instead to a monistic structure of power resulting from a fusion of state and party. Under certain conditions Soviet judges may refuse to enforce administrative decrees; they can never invalidate enactments by the Supreme Soviet. If the Prokuratura is entitled to correct violations of socialist legality by the courts, this amounts to an administrative control of judicial activities; it is not a judicial scrutiny of acts by the legislature or the executive. Hence the Communist systems make explicit what some of the authoritarian Latin American and African regimes practice: promises of their constitutions notwithstanding, the courts in many of these countries do not in fact exercise any review powers.

LAW AND MODERNIZATION

One of the associate justices of the U.S. Supreme Court reflected recently:

---

although legal institutions have educative functions and may reinforce certain interests and weaken others, they have only marginal influence in effecting significant and enduring legal and social change . . . basic change, at least in a country like ours, occurs only with changes in the social order.[33]

As far as Justice White's insight holds true, it applies not only to the United States, but to other countries as well. The relationship between law and social change—and modernization is little else than a new term for social change—needs particular attention when one wishes to view legal developments from a cultural perspective. Two errors have to be avoided. One can of course expect too much from law, as Jeremy Bentham and other reformers did. When a gap develops between legal prescriptions and deeply engrained attitudes and beliefs, the law will fail to change behavior. The ensuing tension between norms and behavior can endanger the community; at the very least law will not bring about change. The fate of the Prohibition Amendment in the United States is there to demonstrate that such an occurrence is not limited to underdeveloped nations.

[33] White, 1971, pp. x–xi.

The opposite error is to exaggerate the contention that all formal changes in law are doomed to fail if they ignore restraints which are imposed by custom and culture. If this were so, legal changes would be impossible unless preceded by cultural change; law reform could do nothing except codify custom. This clearly is not so and ignores the fact that throughout history law has been found to "monitor or otherwise regulate the fact or pace" of social change.[34]

At the outset of our study (see above, Chapter 1), we indicated that all present-day legal systems are adopting major features developed by the three legal families of Western origin. As a deliberate process this wholesale borrowing and penetration of legal norms and institutions is clearly imposed upon modernizing societies "from above," that is, by the government. This is true to an even greater extent than at the time of the reception of Roman law in Renaissance Europe or during the imperialist era in the various colonies. Most striking is the substitution of Western dispute institutions for indigenous and traditional institutions. The demise of traditional law is not tantamount to the demise of traditional society, yet one misjudges reality when one expects that cultural influences and traditional modes of thought will necessarily defeat the effectiveness of law introduced "from above." [35] There might be tensions and clashes between the latter and the continuing practices of the community oriented on local and informal standards. But the outcome for the modernization of law and of society is not a foregone conclusion. It is likely to be different according to the relationships which the law wishes to regulate, and it also depends on such factors as location, communications between the capital and outlying rural districts, and social mobility.

Institutions that are deeply rooted in traditions and values, such as the family, the artisan's workshop, and the rural household, will generally be found more resistant to modern law than those sectors of society that are almost exclusively controlled by lawyers, such as commercial transactions, or the relations between the national bureaucracy and its subjects. Here norms are defined in writing and with great precision where previous rules were oral and vague. In modernizing societies the legal profession, attorneys as well as judges, has a close affinity to the national oligarchy whose interests are served by a centrally administered law.[36] Promoters of new legislation may be intent on generating rules that can be counted upon to induce attitudes furthering modernization. However, the modernizers may not know what those rules are: the more heterogeneous a society, the more

---

[34] Friedman, 1969, p. 29; see also pp. 41ff. for excellent remarks on the problems discussed here.

[35] Bozeman, 1971, defends the opposite thesis.

[36] The role of training and other factors in transforming traditional dispute settlers into something approaching a modern judiciary is interestingly discussed by Abel, 1974, pp. 248ff.

remote will the political and legal elite be from the people to whom the norms are addressed. Yet even in seemingly more homogeneous and more highly developed societies one frequently finds considerable distance between the goals of official or lawyers' law and the habits of daily life in urban ghettoes, impoverished villages and other pockets of society. A progressive integration of groups and relationships, previously untouched by the official law, is everywhere one of the earmarks of legal modernization.

To be uniform in its application modern law must have territorial validity rather than being based on differences in personal status. Correspondingly, rights, obligations, and sanctions must arise from transactions and deeds, such as contracts, torts, or crimes, rather than from one's position in society.[37] Only where this is achieved can ultimate loyalty be transferred from groups of all kinds to the larger national system. The strongest influence for the dissemination of official law and thereby of new loyalties is a hierarchically ordered court system, manned whenever possible by legal experts. Except in harshly totalitarian systems autonomous local dispute settlers will not altogether be deprived of their functions; the question is rather to what extent can they be made responsive to a wider society. Where important judicial norms have not had the strength to penetrate the national system deeply enough, the judiciary has sometimes been overcome by strains which such centrifugal forces as tribalism or localism have produced.[38] Yet there are also examples which prove that a national legal system can leave a particularistic subsystem alone as long as it does not interfere with essentials. If the Habsburg monarchy eventually collapsed it was not because its law could not reach the village communities of ethnic minorities. Today, the official Indian law, representing the values of the anglicized classes, does not determine the conduct of millions of Hindus.[39] Even the Soviet Union has abandoned attempts to alter the traditional and resilient family law of the Islamic population in Central Asia.

The situation which obtains in rapidly modernizing systems is sometimes characterized as giving rise to a "dual law." It is probably better understood as the outcome of an ambiguity toward all legal norms and institutions, an attitude from which no society is entirely free as we have seen. Within limits such an ambiguity is far from being wholly detrimental. It might have the same dynamic function which the economist Albert Hirschman attributes to unbalanced economic growth. Admittedly, the results of

---

[37] On the general role of law in modernization, see Galanter, 1966, pp. 153–65; Coleman, 1968, especially p. 400; and Seidman, 1972, pp. 331ff. with an excellent bibliography.

[38] See Braibanti, 1968, p. 14, with examples drawn from the Pakistani experience.

[39] See Rudolph and Rudolph, 1967, p. 291.

economic performance are easier to determine than the impact of legal developments. Yet it appears that brutal interference with local customs and traditional sanctions might be as dysfunctional for a modernizing legal system as the elimination of time-consuming work ritual was found to be for factory output.[40] An appropriate mitigation of the official law on the local or regional level could help rather than hinder the flexibility required by the overall process of modernization. While parochial interests cannot be permitted to prevail forever, they might still assert themselves in the interstices of official law by such devices as selective nonenforcement, planned inefficiency, and mild corruption. All this can be done "while maintaining the fiction that the law is uniform and unvarying."[41] In an ambiguous situation influences travel both ways; under the best of conditions modernity and tradition achieve a symbiosis rather than survive as a dual system.

Of course on the way breakdowns have occurred and will occur again. They are likely to result in increased human suffering and to destroy the protections of human freedom promised by the rule of law or its equivalents. Law by itself is unable to prevent such catastrophies. Yet in old established as well as in developing societies the lawyer can occupy a special place which has not always been recognized.[42] He must think of himself as a member of a team committed to the kind of long-term social planning which considers the legal prerequisites of a proposed policy together with its economic and social implications. The lawyer will still assume the special role incumbent upon him as the guardian of justice and of legitimate rights. In countries which seek to modernize rapidly it will be his particular task to moderate the zeal of political leaders and social reformers when they wish to deal cavalierly or ruthlessly with valid interests and forces that stand in their way. Everywhere the "active and enlightened role of the lawyer in the complex process of social engineering is an indispensable and vital aspect of mankind's increasingly urgent and precarious struggle for civilized survival."[43]

---

[40] Hirschman, 1958, pp. 143ff.

[41] Galanter, 1966, p. 163.

[42] What follows here is the summary of the important appeal which Friedmann, 1972, p. 520, addressed to the legal community shortly before his tragic death in the streets of New York.

[43] Ibid. p. 521.

BIBLIOGRAPHY

ABEL, RICHARD. 1974. "A Comparative Theory of Dispute Institutions in Society," *Law and Society Review*, 8, 217–347.

ABEL-SMITH, BRIAN, and ROBERT STEVENS. 1967. *Lawyers and the Courts: a Sociological Study of the English Legal System 1750–1965*. London: Heinemann.

———. 1968. *In Search of Justice: Society and the Legal System*. London: Allen Lane.

ABRAHAM, HENRY J. 1968. *The Judicial Process*. New York: Oxford University Press.

ALMOND, GABRIEL, and SIDNEY VERBA. 1965. *The Civic Culture*. Boston: Little, Brown.

ALSCHULER, ALBERT. 1968. "The Prosecutor's Role in Plea Bargaining," *University of Chicago Law Review*, 36, 50–112.

ARNOLD, THURMAN W. (1935) 1962. *The Symbols of Government*. New York: Harcourt & Brace.

AUBERT, VILHELM. 1969. *Sociology of Law*. Baltimore: Penguin Books.

AUERBACH, JEROLD S. 1971. "Enmity and Amity: Law Teachers and Practitioners, 1900–1922," in Donald Fleming and Bernard Bailyn, eds. *Perspectives in American History*. Cambridge, Mass.: Harvard University; Charles Warren Center for Studies in American History. 551–601.

BAKER, RICHARD D. 1971. *Judicial Review in Mexico: A Study of the Amparo Suit*. Austin: University of Texas Press.

BARKUN, MICHAEL. 1971. "Law and Social Revolution: Millenarianism and the Legal System," *Law and Society Review*, 6, 113–41.

BARRY, DONALD D., and HAROLD J. BERMAN. 1971. "The Jurists," in H. G. Skilling and F. Griffiths, eds, *Interest Groups in Soviet Politics*. Princeton: Princeton University Press. 291–334.

BECKER, THEODORE. 1965. *Political Behavioralism and Modern Jurisprudence*. Chicago: Rand McNally.

———. 1970. *Comparative Judicial Politics*. Chicago: Rand McNally.

———, ed. 1971. *Political Trials*. Indianapolis: Bobbs-Merrill.

BEER, SAMUEL H., and ADAM B. ULAM, eds. 1973. *Patterns of Government: the Major Political Systems of Europe*, 3rd ed. New York: Random House.

BENDIX, REINHARD. 1964. *Nation Building and Citizenship*. New York: John Wiley.

————. *The Few and the Many.* To be published by the University of California Press.

BERLE, ADOLPH A., and GARDINER C. MEANS. 1932. *The Modern Corporation and Private Property.* New York: Macmillan.

BERMAN, HAROLD J. 1959. "The Comparison of Soviet and American Law," *Indiana Law Journal,* 34, 559–70.

BLUMENTHAL, MONICA D., ROBERT L. KAHN, FRANK M. ANDREWS, and KENDRA B. HEAD. 1972. *Justifying Violence: Attitudes of American Men.* Ann Arbor: University of Michigan; Institute for Social Research.

BOGNETTI, GIOVANNI, 1973. "The Political Role of the Italian Constitutional Court," unpublished paper presented to the IXth World Congress of the International Political Science Association, Montreal.

BORDUA, DAVID J. 1968. "Police," in *International Encyclopedia of the Social Sciences,* 12, New York: Macmillan. 174–181.

BOZEMAN, ADDA B. 1971. *The Future of Law in a Multicultural World.* Princeton: Princeton University Press.

BRAIBANTI, RALPH. 1968. "The Role of Political Development," in R. Wilson, ed., *International and Comparative Law of the Commonwealth.* Durham, N.C.: Duke University Press.

CAPPELLETTI, MAURO, and JOHN C. ADAMS. 1966. "Judicial Review of Legislation: European Antecedents and Adaptations," *Harvard Law Review,* 79, 1207–24.

————. JOHN H. MERRYMAN, and JOSEPH PERILLO. 1967. *The Italian Legal System: An Introduction.* Stanford: Stanford University Press.

CARDOZO, BENJAMIN. (1921) 1971. *The Nature of the Judicial Process.* New Haven: Yale University Press.

CASAMAYOR. 1970. *Si J'étais Juge.* . . . Paris: Arthaud.

————. 1973*a. La Police.* Paris: Gallimard.

————. 1973*b* . "La Justice et L'Image de L'État," *Le Monde,* July 31.

————. 1973*c.* "L'École des Juges: Entre la Peur et L'Espoir," *Le Monde,* November 3.

CASPER, GERHARD, and HANS ZEISEL. 1972. "Lay Judges in the German Criminal Courts," *The Journal of Legal Studies,* 1. 135–91.

CASPER, JONATHAN D. 1972. *American Criminal Justice: The Defendant's Perspective.* Englewood Cliffs, N.J.: Prentice-Hall.

CHAPMAN, BRIAN. 1970. *Police State.* New York: Praeger.

COHEN, JEROME A. 1968. *Criminal Process in the Peoples' Republic of China, 1949–63.* Cambridge, Mass.: Harvard University Press.

COHEN, MORRIS. 1931. "Fictions," in *Encyclopedia of the Social Sciences,* VI. New York: Macmillan. 225–29.

————. 1940. "Moral Aspects of the Criminal Law," *Yale Law Journal,* 49, 987–1026.

COLE, TAYLOR. 1959. "Three Constitutional Courts—A Comparison," *American Political Science Review,* 53, 963–84.

COLEMAN, JAMES S. 1968. "Modernization: Political Aspects," in *International Encyclopedia of the Social Sciences,* 10. New York: Macmillan, 395–402.

CONQUEST, ROBERT. 1968. *Justice and the Legal System in the U.S.S.R.* New York: Praeger.

CORWIN, EDWARD S. (1929) 1959. *The "Higher Law" Background of American Constitutional Law.* Ithaca: Great Seal Books.

COWAN, PAUL. 1973. "The New Grand Jury," *New York Times Magazine*, April 29, pp. 19 and 34ff.

DAHL, ROBERT A. 1967. *Pluralist Democracy in the United States*. Chicago: Rand Mc-Nally.

DAHRENDORF, RALF. 1964. "The Education of an Elite: Law Faculties and the German Upper Classes," in *Transactions of the Fifth World Congress of Sociology*. Louvain: International Sociological Association.

DANIELSKI, DAVID J. 1969, "The People and the Courts in Japan," in Joel Grossman and Joseph Tanenhaus, eds., *Frontiers of Judicial Research*. New York: John Wiley. 45–72.

————. 1973. "The Political Impact of the Japanese Supreme Court," unpublished paper presented at the IXth World Congress of the International Political Science Association, Montreal.

DAVID, RENÉ, and JOHN E. C. BRIERLEY. 1968. *Major Legal Systems in the World Today: An Introduction to the Comparative Study of Law*. London: Stevens.

DEVINE, DONALD D. 1972. *The Political Culture in the United States*. Boston: Little, Brown.

DEVLIN, PATRICK. 1965. *The Enforcement of Morals*. London: Oxford University Press.

DEWEY, JOHN. 1924. "Logical Method and Law," *Cornell Law Review*, 10, 17–27.

DICEY, ALBERT VENN. (1905) 1926. *Lectures on the Relation between Law and Public Opinion in England During the Nineteenth Century*. New York: Macmillan.

DOLBEARE, KENNETH M. 1967. "The Public Views the Supreme Court," in Herbert Jacob, ed., *Law, Politics and the Federal Courts*. Boston: Little, Brown.

DOUGLAS, WILLIAM O. 1949. "Stare Decisis," *Columbia Law Review*, 49. 735–58.

ECKHOFF, THORSTEIN. 1966. "The Mediator, the Judge and the Administrator in Conflict Resolution," *Acta Sociologica*, 10, 158–66.

EHRENZWEIG, ALBERT. 1959. *Comparative Jurisprudence*. Unpublished material for the use of students at the University of California, Berkeley.

————. 1971. *Psychoanalytic Jurisprudence on Ethics, Aesthetics and "Law"—On Crime, Tort and Procedure*. Dobbs Ferry, N.Y.: Oceana.

EHRLICH, EUGEN. (1912) 1936. *Fundamental Principles of the Sociology of Law*. Trans. by Walter L. Moll. Cambridge, Mass.: Harvard University Press.

EHRMANN, HENRY W. 1971. *Politics in France*. 2nd ed. Boston: Little, Brown.

FEIFER, GEORGE. 1964. *Justice in Moscow*. New York: Simon & Schuster.

FELLMAN, DAVID. 1968. "Domestic Adjudication," in *International Encyclopedia of the Social Sciences*, 1. New York: Macmillan. 42–49.

FINER, MORRIS. 1970. "The Legal Profession," in Michael Zander, ed., *What's Wrong with the Law?*. London: British Broadcasting Company.

FRAENKEL, ERNST. (1927) 1968. "Zur Soziologie der Klassenjustiz," in *Zur Soziologie der Klassenjustiz und Aufsaetze zur Verfassungskrise, 1931–1932*. Darmstadt: Wissenschaftliche Buchgesellschaft. 1–41.

FRANK, JEROME. (1930) 1963. *Law and the Modern Mind*. Garden City, N.Y.: Doubleday.

————. 1956. "Civil Law Influences on the Common Law," *University of Pennsylvania Law Review*, 104, 887–926.

FRIEDMAN, LEON. 1969. "Legal Culture and Social Development," *Law and Society Review*, 6, 19–46.

FRIEDMANN, WOLFGANG. 1967. *Legal Theory,* 5th ed. New York: Columbia University Press.

————. 1972. *Law in a Changing Society,* 2nd ed. New York: Columbia University Press.

FULLER, LON L. 1961. "The Adversary System," in Harold J. Berman, ed., *Talks on American Law.* New York: Vintage Books.

GADBOIS, J. G. 1970. "Indian Legal Behavior," *Economic and Political Weekly,* 5, 149–66.

GALANTER, MARC. 1966. "The Modernization of Law," in Myron Weiner, ed., *Modernization: The Dynamics of Growth.* New York: Basic Books. 153–65.

GELLHORN, WALTER. 1966. *Ombudsmen and Others: Citizens' Protectors in Nine Countries.* Cambridge, Mass.: Harvard University Press.

GLUCKMAN, MAX. 1955. *The Judicial Process among the Barotse of Northern Rhodesia.* Glencoe, Ill.: The Free Press.

GROSSMAN, JOEL B. and JOSEPH TANENHAUS, eds. 1969. *Frontiers of Judicial Research.* New York: John Wiley.

————, and AUSTIN SARAT. 1971. "Political Culture and Judicial Research," *Washington University Law Quarterly,* 2, 177–207.

————. 1973. "Courts and Conflict Resolution." Unpublished paper presented to the IXth World Congress of the International Political Science Association, Montreal.

HAHM, PYONG-CHOON. 1969. "The Decision Process in Korea," in G. A. Schubert and D. J. Danielski, eds., *Comparative Judicial Behavior.* New York: Oxford University Press. 19–48.

HAZARD, JOHN N. 1960. *Settling Disputes in Soviet Society.* New York: Columbia University Press.

————. 1969. *Communists and Their Law.* Chicago: University of Chicago Press.

HENDERSON, DAN FENNO. 1968. "Law and Political Modernization in Japan," in Robert Ward, ed., *Political Development in Modern Japan.* Princeton: Princeton University Press. 387–456.

HIRSCHMAN, ALBERT O., 1958. *The Strategy of Economic Development.* New Haven: Yale University Press.

HOEBEL, EDWARD A. 1954. *The Law of Primitive Man.* Cambridge, Mass.: Harvard University Press.

HOLMES, OLIVER WENDELL. 1881. *The Common Law.* Cambridge, Mass.: Harvard University Press.

HURST, JAMES W. 1950. *The Growth of American Law.* Boston: Little, Brown.

————. 1971. "Legal Elements in United States History," in Donald Fleming and Bernard Bailyn, eds., *Perspectives in American History, III.* Cambridge, Mass.: Harvard University; Charles Warren Center for Studies in American History. 3–92.

JACKSON, RICHARD MEREDITH. 1967. *The Machinery of Justice in England,* 5th ed. Cambridge: Cambridge University Press.

————. 1971. *Enforcing the Law.* Harmondsworth: Penguin.

JAFFE, LOUIS L. 1937. "Law Making of Private Groups," *Harvard Law Review,* 51, 201–53.

————. 1969. *English and American Judges as Lawmakers.* Oxford: Clarendon Press.

JOHNSON, RICHARD M. 1967. *The Dynamics of Compliance: Supreme Court Decision-Making in a New Perspective*. Evanston: Northwestern University Press.

KAHN-FREUND, OTTO. 1962. "English and American Law," in R. A. Newman, ed., *Essays in Jurisprudence in Honor of Roscoe Pound*. American Society for Legal History. 362–409.

KALVEN, HARRY (JR.), and HANS ZEISEL. 1966. *The American Jury*. Boston: Little, Brown.

KAWASHIMA, TAKEYOSHI. 1963. "Dispute Resolution in Contemporary Japan," in A. T. Von Mehren, ed., *Law in Japan: The Legal Order of a Changing Society*. Cambridge, Mass.: Harvard University Press. 41–72.

KESSLER, MARIE-CHRISTINE. 1968. *Le Conseil D'Etat*. Paris: Colin.

KIRCHHEIMER, OTTO. 1961. *Political Justice*. Princeton: Princeton University Press.

KOMMERS, DONALD P. 1969. "The Federal Constitutional Court in the West German Political System," in J. B. Grossman and J. Tanenhaus, eds., *Frontiers of Judicial Research*. New York: John Wiley. 73–132.

———. 1970. "Cross-National Comparisons of Constitutional Courts: Toward a Theory of Judicial Review." Unpublished paper presented to the 66th Annual Meeting of the American Political Science Association, Los Angeles.

———. 1972. "American Civil Liberties and Constitutional Change," *Jahrbuch des Öffentlichen Rechts der Gegenwart*, 21, 603–28.

———. 1975. "Comparative Judicial Review and Constitutional Politics," *World Politics*, 27, 282–97.

LASKI, HAROLD. 1932. "Judiciary," in *Encyclopedia of the Social Sciences*, VIII. New York: Macmillan. 464–94.

LÉVI-STRAUSS, CLAUDE. 1963. *Structural Anthropology*. Trans. by Claire Jacobson and Brooke Grundfest Schoepf. New York: Basic Books.

LUBMAN, STANLEY. 1967. "Mao and Meditation: Politics and Dispute Resolution in Communist China," *California Law Review*, 56, 1284–1359.

McCLOSKEY, HERBERT W. 1964. "Consensus and Ideology in American Politics," *American Political Science Review*, 58, 361–382.

McILWAIN, CHARLES H. 1947. *Constitutionalism, Ancient and Modern*. Ithaca, N.Y.: Cornell University Press.

McWHINNEY, EDWARD. 1965. *Judicial Review*. Toronto: University of Toronto Press.

———. 1974. "Legal Eclecticism and the Development of a Bicultural Canadian Jurisprudence," in A. Popovici, ed., *Problèmes de Droit Contemporain, Mélanges Louis Baudouin*. Montreal: Presses de l'Université de Montréal. 503–570.

MAINE, SIR HENRY SUMNER. (1861) 1916. *Ancient Law*, 10th ed. London: John Murray.

MALINOWSKI, BRONISLAW. 1931. "Culture," in *Encyclopedia of the Social Sciences*, IV. New York: Macmillan. 621–45.

MARCH, JAMES G. (1956) 1964. "Sociological Jurisprudence," in Glendon A. Schubert, ed., *Judicial Behavior*. Chicago: Rand McNally. 132–52.

MAYHEW, LEON. 1968. "Law: The Legal System," in *International Encyclopedia of the Social Sciences*, 9. New York: Macmillan. 51–66.

MENDELSON, WALLACE. 1968. "Judicial Discretion," in *International Encyclopedia of the Social Sciences*, 8. New York: Macmillan. 320–22.

MERRYMAN, JOHN HENRY. 1969. *The Civil Law Tradition*. Stanford: Stanford Uniiversity Press.

MONTESQUIEU, CHARLES LOUIS DE SECONDAT, BARON DE. (1753) 1949. *The Spirit of the Laws.* Trans. by Thomas Nugent. New York: Hafner.

MORIONDO, EZIO. (1966) 1969. "The Value System of Italian Judges," in Vilhelm Aubert, ed., *Sociology of Law.* Baltimore: Penguin. 310–20.

MORRISON, FRED L. 1969. "The Swiss Federal Courts: Judicial Decision-Making and Recruitment," in J. B. Grossman and J. Tanenhaus, eds., *Frontiers of Judicial Research.* New York: John Wiley. 133–62.

MOTE, FREDERICK W. 1968. "Chinese Political Thought," in *International Encyclopedia of the Social Sciences,* 2. New York: Macmillan. 394–408.

MURPHY, WALTER. 1968. "Judicial Values," in *International Encyclopedia of the Social Sciences,* 8. New York: Macmillan. 315–19.

———, and JOSEPH TANENHAUS. 1972. *The Study of Public Law.* New York: Random House.

NADELMANN, KURT H. 1959. "The Judicial Dissent," *American Journal of Comparative Law,* 4, 415–32.

NEUMANN, FRANZ. 1942. *Behemoth: The Structure and Practice of National Socialism.* New York: Oxford University Press.

NEWMAN, DONALD J. 1966. *Conviction: The Determination of Guilt or Innocence Without Trial.* Boston: Little, Brown.

NONET, PHILLIPE, and JEROME CARLIN. 1968. "The Legal Profession," in *International Encyclopedia of the Social Sciences,* 9. New York: Macmillan. 66–72.

NORTHROP, FILMER STUART CUCKROW. 1959. *The Complexity of Legal and Ethical Experience.* Boston: Little, Brown.

PACKER, HERBERT L. 1964. "Two Models of the Criminal Process," *University of Pennsylvania Law Review,* 113, 1–68.

PATON, GEORGE W. 1972. *A Text-Book of Jurisprudence,* 4th ed. Oxford: Clarendon Press.

PEKELIS, ALEXANDER. 1950. *Law and Social Action: Selected Essays.* Ithaca: Cornell University Press.

PELTASON, J. W. 1968. "Judicial Process: Introduction," in *International Encyclopedia of the Social Sciences,* 8. 283–91.

PLATO (ca. 350 B.C.) 1961. "Laws," trans. by A. E. Taylor in Edith Hamilton and Huntington Cairns, eds., *Plato: The Collected Dialogues.* New York: Pantheon Books.

POSPISIL, LEOPOLD. 1967. "Legal Levels and Multiplicity of Legal Systems in Human Societies," *Journal of Conflict Resolution,* 11, 1–26.

PYE, LUCIAN, and SIDNEY VERBA, eds. 1965. *Political Culture and Political Development.* Princeton: Princeton University Press.

RADBRUCH, GUSTAV. 1936. "Anglo-American Jurisprudence through Continental Eyes," *Law Quarterly Review,* 52, 530–545.

———. 1950. *The Legal Philosophies of Lask, Radbruch and Dabin.* Trans. by K. Wilk. Cambridge, Mass.: Harvard University Press.

———. 1956. *Rechtsphilosophie,* 5th ed. Stuttgart: Koehler.

RADCLIFFE-BROWN, ALFRED REGINALD. 1952. *Structure and Function in Primitive Society: Essays and Addresses.* London: Cohen and West.

RHEINSTEIN, MAX. 1968. "Legal Systems: Comparative Law and Legal Systems," in *International Encyclopedia of the Social Sciences,* 9. New York: Macmillan. 204–10.

RIESMAN, DAVID. 1954. *Individualism Reconsidered, and Other Essays.* Glencoe, Ill.: Free Press.

RIEGEL, MANFRED, WERLE, RAYMOND, WILDENMANN, RUDOLF, 1974. *Selbstverstäendnis und Politisches Bewusstsein der Juristen insbesondere der Richterschaft in der Bundesrepublik.* Mannheim: Institut füer Sozialwissenschaften der Universitäet Mannheim.

ROSSITER, CLINTON L. 1948. *Constitutional Dictatorship: Crisis Government in the Modern Democracies.* Princeton: Princeton University Press.

RUDOLPH, LLOYD I. and RUDOLPH SUSANNE HOEBER, 1967. *The Modernity of Tradition.* Chicago: Chicago University Press.

RUSSELL, PETER V. 1969. *The Supreme Court of Canada as a Bilingual and Bicultural Institution.* Document of the Royal Commission on Bilingualism and Biculturalism. Ottowa: Information Canada.

SCHLESINGER, RUDOLPH. 1959. *Comparative Law: Cases, Texts, Materials,* 2nd ed. Brooklyn: Foundation Press.

SCHMIDT, FOLKE F., and STIG STRÖMHOLM. 1964. *Legal Values in Modern Sweden.* Totowa, N.J.: Bedminster Press.

SCHUBERT, GLENDON A. 1967. "Judges and Political Leadership," in Lewis J. Edinger, ed., *Political Leadership in Industrialized Societies.* New York: John Wiley. 220–65.

————. 1968. "Judicial Behavior," in *International Encyclopedia of the Social Sciences,* 8. New York: Macmillan. 307–15.

SCHURMANN, HERBERT FRANZ. 1968. "Chinese Society," in *International Encyclopedia of the Social Sciences,* 2. New York: Macmillan. 408–425.

SEAGLE, WILLIAM. 1932. "Jury: Other Countries," in *Encyclopedia of the Social Sciences,* VIII. New York: Macmillan. 498–502.

————. 1941. *The Quest for Law.* New York: Knopf.

————. 1952. *Law: The Science of Inefficiency.* New York: Macmillan.

SEIDMAN, ROBERT B. 1972. "Law and Development: A General Model," *Law and Society,* 6, 311–42.

SELZNICK, PHILIP. 1968. "Law: The Sociology of Law," in *International Encyclopedia of the Social Sciences,* 9. New York: Macmillan. 50–59.

SINGER, MILTON B. 1968. "The Concept of Culture," in *International Encyclopedia of the Social Sciences,* 3. New York: Macmillan. 527–43.

SKILLING, HAROLD GORDON, and FRANKLYN GRIFFITHS, eds. 1971. *Interest Groups in Soviet Politics.* Princeton: Princeton University Press.

SOLZHENITSYN, ALEKSANDR I. 1974. *The Gulag Archipelago, 1918–1956.* New York: Harper & Row.

STEVENS, ROBERT. 1971. "Two Cheers for 1871: The American Law School," in Donald Fleming and Bernard Bailyn, eds., *Perspectives in American History.* Cambridge, Mass,: Harvard University; Charles Warren Center for Studies in American History. 405–548.

STONE, JULIUS. 1966. *Social Dimensions of Law and Justice.* Stanford: Stanford University Press.

TOCQUEVILLE, ALEXIS DE. (1835) 1957. *Democracy in America.* Trans. by Henry Reeve, rev. by Francis Bonen. New York: Vintage Books.

————. (1856) 1955. *The Old Regime and the French Revolution.* Trans. by Stuart Gilbert. Garden City: Doubleday.

TORGERSON, ULF. 1963. "The Role of the Supreme Court in the Norwegian Political System," in Glendon A. Schubert, ed., *Judicial Decision Making*. New York: The Free Press of Glencoe. 221–44.

ULMER, S. SIDNEY. 1971. *Courts as Small and Not So Small Groups*. New York: General Learning Press.

VERBA, SIDNEY. 1965. "Conclusion: Comparative Political Culture," in L. Pye and S. Verba, eds., *Political Culture and Political Development*. Princeton: Princeton University Press. 512–60.

VINES, KENNETH N. 1969. "The Judicial Role in the American States: An Exploration," in J. B. Grossman and J. Tanenhaus, eds., *Frontiers of Judicial Research*. New York: John Wiley. 461–85.

VON MEHREN, ARTHUR TAYLOR. 1957. *The Civil Law System: Cases and Materials for the Comparative Study of Law*. Boston: Little, Brown.

——, ed. 1963. *Law in Japan: The Legal Order in a Changing Society*. Cambridge, Mass.: Harvard University Press.

WARREN, SAMUEL D., and LOUIS D. BRANDEIS. 1890. "The Right to Privacy," *Harvard Law Review*, 4, 193–220.

WASBY, STEVEN L. 1973. "The U.S. Supreme Court's Impact: Broadening Our Focus." Paper presented at the IXth World Congress of the International Political Science Association, Montreal.

WEAVER, WARREN JR. 1973. "Support of High Court up among Police and Public," *New York Times*, July 29, pp. 1 and 31.

WEBER, MAX. (1922) 1954. *Law in Economy and Society*, 2nd ed. Trans. by Edward Shils and Max Rheinstein. Cambridge, Mass.: Harvard University Press.

WEINER, MYRON. 1965. "India: Two Political Cultures," in L. Pye and S. Verba, eds., *Political Culture and Political Development*. Princeton: Princeton University Press. 199–244.

WERLE, RAYMOND. 1973. "The Perception of Judicial Independence and the Function of Judges in the Regular Courts in the Federal Republic of Germany." Unpublished paper presented to the IXth World Congress of the International Political Science Association, Montreal.

WEYRAUCH, WALTER O. 1964. *The Personality of Lawyers: A Comparative Study of Subjective Factors in Law*. New Haven: Yale University Press.

WHITE, BYRON. 1971. "Preface," in D. Fleming and B. Bailyn, eds., *Perspectives in American History*. Cambridge, Mass.: Harvard University; Charles Warren Center for Studies in American History. V–XI.

WILDENMANN, RUDOLPH. 1973. "Attitudes of Judges as a Subject for Comparative Study." Unpublished paper presented to the IXth World Congress of the International Political Science Association, Montreal.

WILLIAMS, PHILIP M., and MARTIN HARRISON. 1971. *Politics and Society in De Gaulle's Republic*. London: Longmans.

ZEIDLIN, THEODORE. 1973. *France 1848–1945. Vol. 1*. Oxford: Clarendon Press.

INDEX